Jan Messent's

Knit A Fantasy Story

SEARCH PRESS
Classics

Published in Great Britain as *Jan Messent's Knit a Fantasy Story* 2006
Search Press Limited,
Wellwood, North Farm Road
Tunbridge Wells, Kent TN2 3DR

Originally published in 1989 as *Knit a Fantasy Story*

In association with
Child & Associates Pty Ltd
5 Skyline Place
Frenches Forest
NSW, Australia 2086
   and
David Bateman Ltd
Golden Heights
32-34 View Road
Glenfield
Auckland, New Zealand

Copyright © Search Press Ltd 1989, 2006

Based on the following volumes of the Craft Library series, published
by Search Press Limited:
The Knitted Farmyard. Original German version *Spiellandschaft aus
Wolle* (No 200 in the Brunnen-Reihe series) copyright © 1982
Christophorus-Verlag Gmbh, Freiburg im Breisgau. English version
copyright © 1985 Search Press Limited. Original text and designs
by Hannelore Wernhard; translated by Hilary Simpson, rewritten and
with new drawings by Jan Messent;
photographs by Ulrike Schneiders.

Knit an Enchanted Castle by Jan Messent

Knitted Gnomes and Fairies by Jan Messent

ISBN 978-1-84448-181-1

Printed in Malaysia by Times Offset (m) Sdn Bhd

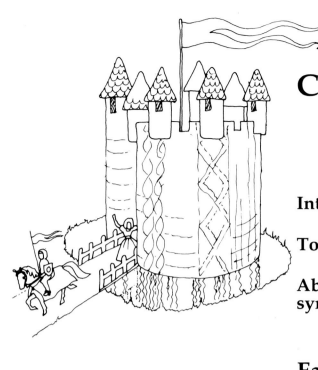

CONTENTS

INTRODUCTION

Enter a world of make-believe; an enchanted world of witches and wizards, fairies and goblins, bold knights, dragons, trolls and unicorns. The sleepy little farm nestles snugly under the hills, looking out over the enchanted forest, where fairies and gnomes work and play. Inside the huge stone castle lives the handsome prince, who will one day find his beautiful princess and take her to live there in safety, far away from the mischievous plottings of the wicked witch.

Well, that's the beginning of the story!

What happens along the way can be made with the help of an active imagination, these patterns and a little time and patience. Fairy stories are as popular today as they have ever been in the past, delighting both children and adults. Naturally, your attempt to create this enchanted land must rely partly on your own ideas and partly on suggestions found in literature and art. We have made this book of make-believe in a truly three-dimensional way to delight anyone with a sense of fantasy and fun.

The scale of the models is probably the most important element of the project, so seek out your finest needles, hooks and yarn and enjoy working in miniature. The tallest of the figures is approximately 5 in/14 cm tall. The base of the farm is the size of a small rug, although it can be made larger if you wish. The castle rises 16 in/41 cm to the tops of the pointed roofs and its base is the size of a large dinner plate.

The farm is built up using a mixture of knitting and crochet, although all the main pieces are knitted. The quantities of materials required are quite small; oddments of knitting yarns, rug canvas and embroidery threads, synthetic padding and pipe cleaners. The enchanted castle and the forest are made out of wool, cardboard tubes, card and wire.

All the figures are based on a wire frame and therefore make unsuitable toys for very young children, as they may be dangerous if not handled carefully. For practical reasons the clothes are not intended to be removed.

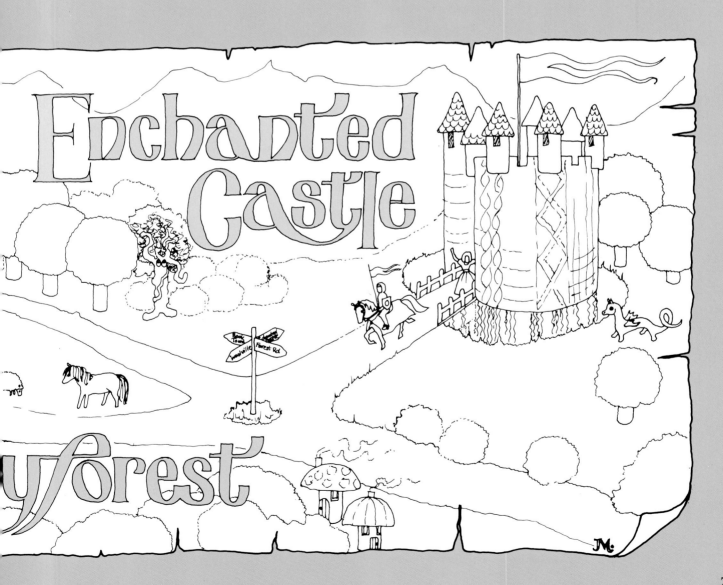

In the patterns they fit tightly without fastenings and the fairy folk have their wings sewn firmly on to their backs, so securing their clothes.

Although most of the knitting is on a small scale the instructions are not complex. The shapes used for body coverings and clothes are simple and are mostly based on rectangles or triangles, with occasional increasing and decreasing. Even the castle is made from straight pieces of knitting and

would be an excellent project for a group of people to make together.

Use your imagination to add props and backgrounds to your enchanted land. Dolls' house accessories would be ideal. Oddments and scraps could add new dimensions to your knitted landscape. Young and old alike will enjoy hours of pleasure and fun while creating this land of fantasy and enchantment.

Specific details of the materials required and the methods of working each figure are given in the instructions but it is impossible to give exact details of the finished sizes, as this will depend on the yarn and needle size you use and the tension you obtain.

Needles

Requirements are given in the instructions for individual models but, generally, very fine needles are used throughout. It is sometimes easier to find these in sets of four double-pointed needles, rather than in pairs. These are perfectly adequate as only a few stitches are used for most projects. Fine Shetland 'wires', also found in sets of four, are used to create some of the garments for the fairy folk.

Other requirements include stitch holders and row counters, blunt-ended needles for sewing with wool, (tapestry needles) and a fine crochet hook.

Yarns

Requirements are given in the instructions for individual models, although the colours are your own personal choice. Only small amounts of two, three and four ply are normally needed but double knitting qualities have been used for the enchanted castle and the forest.

Use the very finest yarns you can find for the fairy folk. Glittering metallic yarns add sparkle and magic to an elf or pixie. Mohair mixtures are suitable for hair and beards and you will also need a thick yarn for wrapping around the frames of the figures. Textured and marbled yarns, such as bouclé and tweed, are ideal for the animals. Oddments of suitable colours will also be required for embroidering features and adding minute details.

The knitted body covering for the inhabitants of the Fantasy Story needs to be worked in a fine, smooth yarn. The illustrations will indicate suitable colouring but if you cannot obtain a pleasing flesh tone, use white two-ply dipped in strong tea or coffee. Wind off a hank, tie it in two or three places to prevent it becoming tangled, then dip in hot or cold tea or coffee for anything from ten to thirty minutes. Keep checking until you have the shade you require but remember that the colour will appear darker when wet.

Wire

Pipe cleaners are used as the basic framework for all the characters and 11in/28cm of thicker, but bendy wire, is needed for the fairy wings. Strong, bendable wire is required for the talking trees. You will also need wire cutters and a small pair of pliers.

Padding and card

Padding is needed for the animals, toadstools, talking trees and to pad out any very stout figures, such as the gnome or goblin. The cardboard tubes inside toilet rolls, also larger tubes approximately 9in/23cm high are needed and small pieces of thick card for stands.

Extras

Pencils and rulers are useful, as are tape measures, glue, adhesive tape (also double-sided), sharp scissors and lots of patience!

All kinds of extras may be added as the fancy takes you. Brighten up the fairy folk with tiny beads and sequins. Buckles, buttons, broken jewellery and gold and silver cord and braid will all add a touch of sparkle, so look in your 'bit box'. Anything small enough will most certainly have a use.

Sizes and tension

Please note that all the instructions given in this book are merely guidelines and will almost certainly have to be altered here and there to fit figures and shapes of all sizes, as no two people ever work to exactly the same tension. You may have to add or subtract a few stitches and/or rows and if a different weight of yarn is used from the one recommended, then a bit of juggling is inevitable!

It is therefore vital to check your knitted pieces against the model you have made, to make sure that each bit fits before the garment is sewn up.

ABBREVIATIONS, STITCHES, SYMBOLS

Most of the items in this book are knitted in stocking stitch, made by knitting and purling alternate rows. The other side of this fabric is known as 'reverse stocking stitch'. Garter stitch is formed by knitting every row.

Other knitting, crochet and general abbreviations are as follows:

alt	alternate(ly)
beg	begin(ning)
cm	centimetre(s)
ch	crochet chains
ch sp	chain space
dec	decrease
dc	double crochet (US, single crochet)
DK	double knitting yarn
foll	following
gt s	garter stitch
gm	gramme(s)
in	inch(es)
inc	increase
k	knit
k 2 tog	knit 2 together to decrease
LH	left hand
k-wise	in a knitwise direction
M1	make 1 by picking up loop
mm	millimetre(s)
No	number
oz	ounce(s)
patt	pattern
pc	pipe cleaner(s)
p	purl
p 2 tog	purl 2 together to decrease
p-wise	in a purlwise direction
psso	pass slipped stitch over
rev ss	reversed stocking stitch
rem	remain(ing)
rep	repeat
RS	right side of fabric
sl	slip
st	stitch(es)
ss	stocking stitch
tog	together
WS	wrong side of fabric
y fwd	yarn forward
yrn	yarn round needle

Stitches used

Double moss stitch
Garter stitch
Moss stitch
Other stitches of own choice
Picot stitch
Reversed stocking stitch
Single rib
Stocking stitch

Symbols used

A single asterisk, *, in the row indicates that the stitches following this sign are to be repeated as directed.

Instructions given in round brackets, ( ), are repeated as many times as indicated in the instructions.

11

FARMYARD FANTASIA

*The farmer and his family work all day
beneath the shade of the magic forest,
protected by the enchanted castle.*

LANDSCAPE

This colourful setting is a wonderful landscape for your farmyard fantasy.

Rug base

Copy the rug diagram opposite, full-scale, on to a large piece of brown paper, and use this as a pattern for the rug canvas work. Place it underneath the canvas and draw on to this with a thick fibre pen. You will need rug canvas measuring 52 × 35½ in/130 × 90 cm, plus an extra 2¼ in/6 cm all round for turning under.

Yarns: thick knitting wools, rug-thrums and cut rug-wool will be most useful for the base, part of which is covered with tufting and some with stitchery (see Figs 1 and 2).

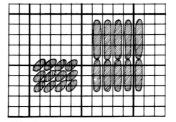

Fig 1:
left, tent stitch
right, satin stitch over
three and four threads
of the canvas

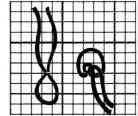

Fig 2:
tufting on rug canvas may
be done with a latchet hook,
or with a crochet hook

COLOURS AND STITCHES

Meadows: pale green 4 in/10 cm lengths of yarn knotted into the canvas as shown in Fig 1.

Street and yard: grey/beige double-thickness yarn embroidered in tent st.

Ploughed fields: several different browns, knitted in single rib to the shapes of the pattern and sewn on to the canvas.

Cornfields: several different yellows, as follows:

Ripe corn: 7 in/18 cm lengths of double yarn in deep yellow, and knotted.

Cornfield 1: knotted with 6¼ in/16 cm lengths of deep green yarn, doubled.

Cornfield 2: two tones of green yarn, 7¾ in/20 cm long, knotted.

Cornfield 3: double yarn in tones of yellow and green, embroidered in tent st.

Cut corn: double yarn in tones of yellow, embroidered in satin st.

Hayfields and stubble: various light and medium greens used 4-fold in a wide satin st for the hayfield. The stubble is worked in double yarn in tent st.

Bushes: deep green yarns, shown as shaded patches in the diagram. Short lengths of yarn are made into pom-pons and sewn on to the fields after these have been stitched.

Stream and pond: two or three different blues used together, embroidered in chain st.

Bridge: knitted in simple rib and stitched over the stream joining the street across the water.

Fig 3: plan of the rug base

Trees

You will need two tubes of cardboard for the inside of the trees; the tops are made of large pom-pons in thick, green yarn. The trunk is knitted as follows: using dark brown yarn on No10/3¼mm needles, knit a piece measuring 5½in/14cm long. Roll this around the cardboard tube and sew it up lengthways. Glue the pom-pon to the top. Each tree will stand more firmly if it is given a base of either tufted canvas or cardboard.

Flowers and plants

These can be knitted, crocheted, or made of tiny tufts of yarn from small oddments. They are extremely simple and can be made without a pattern; just crochet chains and link them together at a central point. These are scattered here and there around the scene, in front of the cottages, and around the trees and bushes.

BUILDINGS

As these can be knitted with any kind of yarn, from a fine 3 ply to thick rug-thrums, no specific instructions have been given regarding needle sizes, stitches or rows. Instead, each knitter should consult the chart opposite and make the building pieces to those measurements. It will be noted that extra buildings appear on some photographs; these have been made from the same pattern. Each building is filled with a block of foam cut to the correct shape. This should be made

The farmer and his wife look out over their fields.

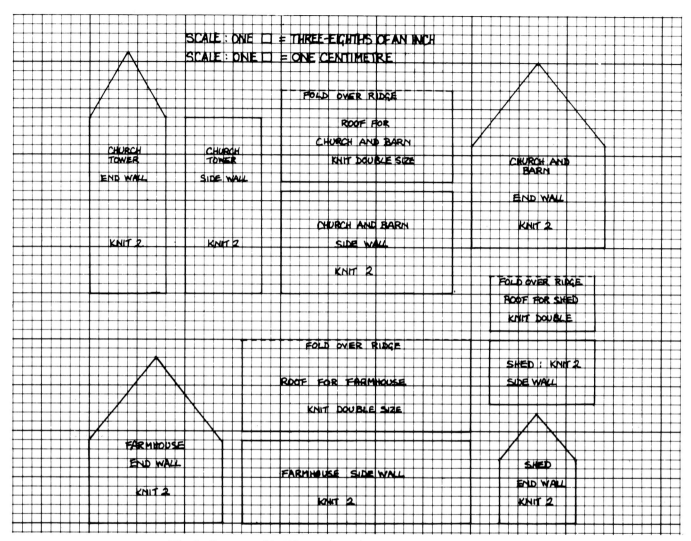

Fig 4: diagram of building patterns seen in many of the illustrations

slightly larger than the knitting to ensure a snug fit. Extra instructions for each building, and materials are given on this page.

Shed

This is the smallest of all the buildings, (see page 36). The walls are knitted in a k1, p2, rib pattern in brown, and the roof is worked in garter st in rust.

Barn

This pattern, (see page 36), is used also for the main part of the church, and for the stable building seen on page 29. The barn is made of dark-brown yarn with beige/rust for the roof, which is knitted in garter st. The walls are knitted in k1, p2 rib. The walls of the other buildings are of stocking st, with a ridge around the base of 6 rows of garter st.

The barn door is made in k1, p1 rib, decreasing at the top to make a curve. The edge is embroidered in chain st to give a crisp finish.

Church

White yarn is used for the main part, (see opposite), and rust-mottled tweed for the roof, with oddments of dark and mid-brown.

Farmhouse

Beige yarn is used for the walls, rust for the roof, and small amounts of other colours for windows and doors (see opposite). The roof is knitted in double rib (k2, p2 on every row) and the walls begin with 6 rows of garter st, before continuing in stocking st.

FIGURES

The materials required are:

6 pipe-cleaners for each figure
Wadding (about ½ yard/metre should be enough for all the figures and animals). Thick pink yarn for binding. Fine 3 ply skin-coloured yarn for knitted body-coverings. (A 1oz/25gm ball will be enough for all the adults and children.) One pair each No13/2¼ mm and No12/2¾ mm needles, crochet hooks, wool needles, scissors and tape-measure.

Basic body

The following instructions are for all the figures; the sizes for the children are given in Fig 9.

Take two pipe-cleaners and lay them end to end overlapping by about ¾ in/2 cm. Twist them together where they overlap, to make one long piece, (see Fig 5). Now do the same with two more, and lay the two pieces side by side. Bend into shape as shown, to make the head, (see Fig 6). Twist the legs gently together and turn the feet up very slightly to make the legs even. Take two more pipe-cleaners and lay them

evenly across the shoulders, twisting them as shown. Turn up the end slightly to shorten the arms, (see Fig 7).

Cover the head and body with a piece of padding, and bind this gently in place with the thick pink yarn, winding it also around the legs and arms to thicken them. Draw the yarn tightly around the neck to define it, (see Fig 8). The children are made in the same way as the adults except that the pipe-cleaner frame is shortened at the hands and feet.

KNITTED BODY COVERING

(*Note.* The farmer's wife is made differently, see page 23). The body-covering for the children is made in the same way as the adults, but you should check the length of each piece against the child's figure before finishing. You may also find that you need one or two less sts than the adult pattern. The little girl wears white ankle socks which should be knitted into the bottom of the legs before the shoes.

Use the No13/2¼ mm needles and the fine skin-coloured yarn. Begin with the main body piece which

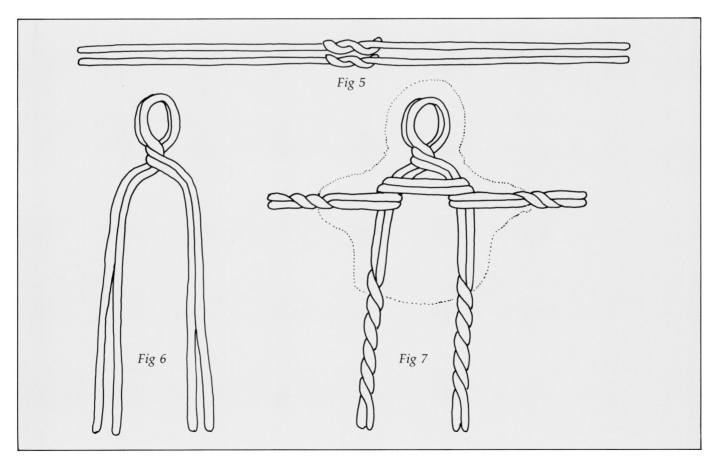

Fig 5

Fig 6

Fig 7

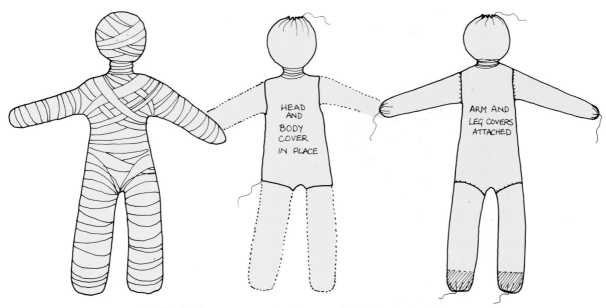

Fig 8: the figure wrapped and covered with the knitted pieces

also covers the head. Cast on 22sts and work in ss for 16 rows from the top of the legs to the under-arm. This should now be checked against the figure framework as sizes will vary depending on yarn, tension and the padding on the body. Now divide for the arms. K6. Turn and work on these 6sts alone for 6 more rows. Break off the yarn. Attach the yarn to the other group of sts and k10. Work on these 10sts alone for 6 more rows. Break off yarn. Attach the yarn to the last group and work 6 more rows, but do not break the yarn. Now continue across all the sts for 13 more rows. (Again, this should be checked against the figure, bearing in mind that the knitting will stretch a little.) Do not cast off; gather the sts on to a threaded wool needle and draw them together. Slip the arms into the holes, and the last sts on top of the head. Sew up the back seam, wrapping the yarn tightly around the neck. At the base, pull the two edges together in the centre between the legs, ready for the leg-pieces to be joined on, (see Fig 8).

Arms

Cast on 10sts and work 18 rows in ss. Check to see whether this piece fits the arms on your figure. K 2 tog all along the next row, then thread the yarn on to the last 5sts and gather up. Slip this on to the arm with the gathers at the hand end, and sew up. Attach the piece around the armhole, and make another piece to match.

Legs

Cast on 10sts and work in ss for the length of the leg as far as the ankle – about 22 rows. If the legs are not as long as you would like them to be, take this opportunity to add more rows at this point and pad the shoe area with wool before sewing up.

The last 6 rows are worked in shoe colour in either ss or gt s. They are finished off in the same way as the hands (the farmer wears separately made boots). Sew the cast-on edge to the bottom of the body covering around the top of the leg.

Make another in the same way, (see Fig 8).

Faces and hair

The hair and beards are embroidered using scraps of brown and fair wool, and the spectacles are made of brass wire. The features are also embroidered on using oddments of yarn.

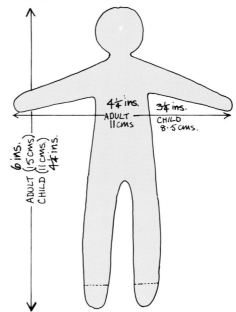

Fig 9: the body measurements after covering

19

The mother and father, two children and baby, and the dog.

Father

Use contrasting oddments of yarn and lots of colours to add interest to the figure.

TROUSERS

Knitted in gt s on size No13/2¼ mm needles in fine 3 ply or 4 ply. Cast on 22sts and knit 26 rows.
Row 27; cast off 12sts and k to end of row (10sts).
Row 28; k10, turn and cast on 12sts. K to end of row (22sts).
Knit across all sts for 25 more rows. Cast off.
Fold the two side edges towards each other and sew up the centre back seam. Now sew up the inside leg seams, (see Fig 10).

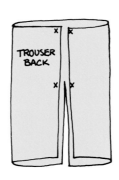

Fig 10: the trouser pattern

SHIRT

The back and front are worked in one piece, with separate sleeves (see above). Use size No12/2¾mm needles, cast on 12sts and work 16 rows in ss.

Next row; k3, cast off 6sts, k to end.

Next row; p3, turn and cast on 3sts, k back to the beg of the row, working into the back of the 4th st. Work 5 more rows on these 6sts ending on a p row. Break off yarn and attach it to the other 3sts, casting on 3 more sts at the same time on the neck edge.

Purl back to the end of the row, working into the back of the 4th st. Work 5 rows on these 6sts ending with a k row, then work across the other 6sts also, to join the two sides.

Next row; p. Work 8 more rows and cast off.

Sleeves

Cast on 15sts and work 2 rows in ss.

Cast off 2sts at beg of next 2 rows.

Next row; k 2 tog, k 7, k 2 tog, (9sts). Cast off p-wise. Make another one the same. Lay the shirt body section out flat and sew the sleeve, centrally positioned, to this. Then sew the underarm and side seams all at once. You may wish to work a row of crochet around the neck to finish it off. The back opening may be stitched up once it is on the figure but to make it easy to remove, you may prefer to attach a tiny button and loop.

RUCKSACK

The rucksack is shown on page 26. Using 3 ply yarn and No13/2¼mm needles, cast on 10sts and work in stocking st for 24 rows.

Dec one st at each end of the next 2 rows, then work 2 more rows. Cast off 6sts. The strap is a crochet chain, and the flap has an edge of crochet to keep it flat. It can be fastened with a press-stud.

Mother

The mother is wearing the same trousers as the father, so follow the pattern on page 20.

PULLOVER

This is made in one piece from one sleeve edge to the other. It opens down the back from neck to hem (see Fig 11).

Use No12/2¾mm needles and 3 ply or 4 ply yarn.

Cast on 16sts and work 12 rows in ss.

Cast on 8 more sts at beg of the next 2 rows, working into the back of the 9th st on each row (32sts). Work 4 more rows, then divide for the neck opening as follows:

K15, cast off 2sts, k to end of row.

Work 3 rows on these 15sts.

Next row; * k2, yarn forward, k 2 tog, * 3 times. K3. This makes 3 buttonholes.

Next row; p, then cast off.

Rejoin the yarn to the other sts and work 8 rows, beg with a p row.

Next row; cast on 17sts, p back across all 32sts, purling into the back of the 18th st.

Work 5 more rows, ending with a p row.

Cast off 8sts at beg of the next 2 rows, and work 12 rows in ss.

Next row; cast off.

Attach 3 tiny buttons to the back opening, and sew up the seams.

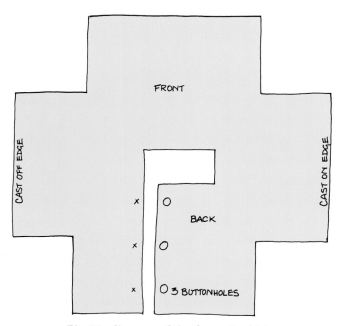

Fig 11: diagram of the farmer's shirt and the mother's pullover

The farmer and his donkey.

Farmer

The same shirt pattern is used as for the mother's pullover, though the colour is different. The trousers are also the same, except that the farmer's have crocheted straps, or braces. The farmer's hat may be knitted or crocheted: here is the knitted version.

HAT

Use 3 ply yarn and size No13/2¼ mm needles: cast on 22sts.
Work 4 rows in ss, then k 2 tog all along the row.
Purl the next row, then gather the rem sts on to a thread and leave. With the right side facing you, pick up 22sts from the cast-on edge and k back, inc into every st.
K 2 rows and then cast off. Sew up the back seam, and make a crochet chain to go around the brim.

BOOTS

Use No13/2¼ mm needles and dark-brown 3 ply yarn.
Cast on 15sts and work 10 rows in ss.
Row 11; p, then work in reversed ss for 6 more rows.
Next row; k 2 tog all along the row to the last st, k1.
Gather up the rem sts on to a length of yarn and sew up. Place a small amount of padding in the toe of the boot and fix on to the foot.

Farmer's wife

The farmer's wife wears a long skirt which is enclosed at the base with an oval-shaped piece of card, so her legs do not need a knitted covering. Unlike the other figures, her clothes are not removable; her dress-bodice and head-covering are made in one piece, as are the sleeves and hands.

BODICE AND HEAD-COVERING

Use size No13/2¼mm needles and dress-coloured yarn.

Cast on 22sts and work in ss for 4 rows. Then divide for the arms: k6, turn, and work on these 6sts for 6 more rows. Cut the yarn and attach it to the other group of sts.

K 10, turn and work on these 10 sts for 6 more rows. Complete as for first section.

Work 6 rows on the next 6sts, then p across all 22sts. Work 4 more rows to finish the neckline.

Change to the skin-coloured yarn, and work in ss for 11 rows. Finish the top of the head as for the other figures.

SLEEVES AND HANDS

These are worked in gt s and ss respectively.

Using dress-coloured yarn, cast on 10sts and k 16 rows.

The farmer's wife, watched by the kitten and the cockerel, picks lettuces.
The stables and trees are in the background.

23

The farmer's wife and her mule.

Change to skin-coloured yarn and ss. Work 4 more rows.

On the 5th row, k 2 tog 5 times.

Gather the rem sts on to a thread and sew the hand and arm seam on the wrong side. Reverse the sleeve and attach to the figure.

SKIRT

Use size No11/3 mm needles and dress-coloured yarn, cast on 25sts and work in gt s for 6¼ in/16 cm. Cast off and sew this edge to the cast-on edge. Gather one edge of the tube and attach it to the bodice. Cut an oval-shaped card for the base of the skirt and stick it in place inside the hem to give a firm base to the figure.

APRON

Use size No14/2 mm needles, pale yarn, cast on 14sts, work 4 rows gt s, then 22 rows ss. Cast off. Gather the top slightly and sew on to the figure. Crochet a long chain about 8in/20cm, and sew this around the waist-line to tie at the back.

HAIR

Cut 6 × 8¾ in/15 × 22 cm lengths of coppery-red yarn and sew these centrally to the middle of the head. Then tie them together at the nape of the neck, securing them there with a few sts. Tie them again further down and sew on to the middle of the head at the top, twisting them into a knot and sewing them down firmly. Embroider the features.

Children

The children's clothes can be knitted up using just a few oddments of brightly coloured yarn.

TROUSERS

These are worked as for the adults, (see pattern page 20), except that they are shorter. Use size No13/2¼ mm needles, cast on 12sts and, to divide for the legs, cast off half the stitches.

JUMPERS

The boy's jumper is knitted in stripes but the instructions are the same as for the father's shirt, except for the sleeves. Each piece should be measured for length against the figure. The girl's jumper is a sleeveless version of the same pattern.

Sleeve for boy's jumper
Cast on 12sts and work 2 rows in ss.
Cast off 2sts at beg of next 2 rows.
Next row; k 2 tog, k 4, k 2 tog, (6sts). Cast off p-wise.

HAIR

The hair of both children is embroidered on to the head in fair and dark yarns; the little girl may have plaits.

The children and their pony, not to mention the dog.

The family enjoys a picnic under the trees.

Baby

The same kind of wire construction is used as for the other figures, but on a much smaller scale. Only three pipe-cleaners are used for the frame, two for the head and body and one bent in half for the arms. Turn the feet and hands up so that the overall length is about 2⅜ in/6 cm and the width across the arms is about 1¾ in/4.5 cm. There is no need to use padding on this small frame, only thick pink yarn to bind it round. The body-covering and rompers are made in one piece in ss, beginning with the head.

KNITTED COVER AND ROMPERS
Use size No13/2¼ mm needles and fine pink yarn, cast on 12sts and work 8 rows. Change to blue yarn and work 2 rows. Now make holes for the arms as follows:

k2, yarn forward, k 2 tog, k 4, yarn forward, k 2 tog, k 2.
Work across all sts making a total of 10 blue rows, then divide for the legs.
K 6 and work on these 6sts for 10 rows. Change to pink yarn and work 4 rows. Leave the sts on a thread. Work the other leg to match. Slip the arms through the two holes and sew up the leg and back seams. Now make the two arms: cast on 6sts in white yarn and work 4 rows. Purl the next row, then change to pink yarn and work 2 rows. Draw the thread through the rem sts and complete as for other arm. Embroider features and a little hair if you wish.

26

ANIMALS

Begin with the simplest and smallest, and work towards the larger and more complicated animals.

Ducks

Cast on 22sts in white yarn and k 3 rows.
4th row; k 2 tog, k to end of row.
Repeat this row 11 more times.
Knit 9 more rows on the rem 10sts. Cast off.
Fold the shape as shown, stuff, and finish off with beak and eyes.

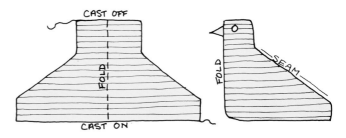

Fig 12: basic and sewn shape for the duck

The little boy and the ducks.

Some hens and a cockerel scratch around the barn.

Hens and cockerels

You will need small amounts of 3 ply or 4 ply yarn in brown, white and red, a very small amount of yellow for the beaks, some brightly coloured embroidery cottons for the cockerel's tail and for his legs. You will need half a pipe-cleaner plus wadding for the bodies. Use size No12/2¾ mm and No11/3 mm needles. All birds are knitted in gt s.

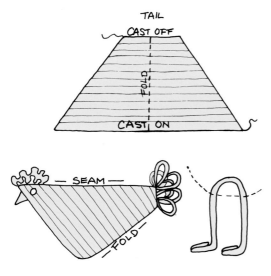

Fig 13: basic shape, sewn shape and legs for the hen

Cast on 18sts in brown yarn and k 3 rows.
4th row; k 2 tog, then k to end of row.
Repeat row 4 until there are only 6sts left. Cast off. Complete as shown in the diagram, making a crochet chain for the tail feathers. The cockerel's tail is larger and more brightly coloured. Use the half pipe-cleaner to make the legs and wrap it round with yarn before stitching into place.

Kitten

The kitten is shown opposite and on page 23.
You will need small oddments of 3 ply or 4 ply yarns in grey, white and black, or any cat colour you wish. Size No12/2¾ mm or No11/3 mm needles. Cast on 8sts in body-colour and work in ss.
Knit 1 row.
2nd row; inc into every st (16sts), then work 8 rows.
Row 11; k 2 tog all along the row (8sts).
Work 6 rows then draw a thread through the sts, pad the shape and sew up. Gather a thread around the neck. Make a tail of 4sts and 10 rows in ss.

Legs
Use size No13/2¼ mm needles, cast on 7sts with white yarn and work 9 rows ss. Make 4.

Ears
Cast on 3sts with black yarn, k 2 rows and cast off. Make 2.

Pig

You will need small amounts of pink or beige yarn. Note that in this version shown below, the legs are made separately from the body. Begin at the back and work towards the nose, using gt s on size No12/2¾ mm or No11/3 mm needles.

Cast on 20sts and k 24 rows.

Now dec on alternate rows as follows:

Row 25; k 7, k 2 tog, k 2, k 2 tog, k 7.

Row 27; k 6, k 2 tog, k 2, k 2 tog, k 6.

Row 29; k 5 and continue in the same manner as above.

Row 31; k 4 ditto.

Work 2 rows straight.

Row 34; k 2 tog, to the end of the row.

Row 35; p and then draw the last sts on to a thread, using this to sew up the body after padding it.

Legs

Use size No14/2 mm needles, cast on 8sts, and work 10 rows ss. Cast off. Fold, pad and join to body. Make 4. Embroider the eyes and make a curly tail of crochet.

The farmer, his pigs and the kitten,
outside the barn on the right and the stable.

Some sheep grazing by the shed.

Sheep

For the body you will need white yarn (bouclé, or curly wool is best), and fawn or black yarn for the faces and legs. You will also need 2 pipe-cleaners for the legs. The body is knitted in gt s, and the faces and legs in ss. You will also need wadding, needle sizes No13/2¼ mm and No11/3 mm, and yarn for the eyes.

Body

Begin at the tail-end, using white yarn and No11/3 mm needles, cast on 18 sts and k 17 rows.

Dec one st at the beg and the end of the next row, and also on row 20 and 22.

Row 23; change to No14/2 mm needles and fawn or black yarn and work 8 rows in ss (this is the nose). Draw the rem sts on to a length of yarn, pad the cavity and sew it up with the seam underneath.

Legs

Take 2 pipe-cleaners and fold them in half. Now curve them round and insert one end into one side of the body and out at the other, through the knitting where one pair of legs should be. Do the same for the other pair, then bend the wire up so that it is 4-fold and half

as long. The knitted leg covering can now be slipped over these and sewn in place.

Using size No13/2¼ mm needles and fawn or black yarn, cast on 8sts and work 10 rows. Draw up the sts at the foot, and make 3 more pieces the same.

Ears

With No14/2 mm needles, white yarn, cast on 3sts, and work 5 rows. Do not cast off. Draw sts up and sew on with rem thread. Make 2.

Dog

Instead of being crocheted, as in the photograph below, this version is knitted and the legs are made separately from the body. It will, however, look more or less the same as the one illustrated.

You will need small amounts of white 3 ply or 4 ply yarn, and tan for the spots and ears, 4 pipe-cleaners for the frame, padding and a thick yarn for binding. Also, size No13/2¼ mm needles.

Make the frame as shown in the diagram overleaf,

The farmer cuts hay and the boy rakes it up.
Their tools lean against the shed.

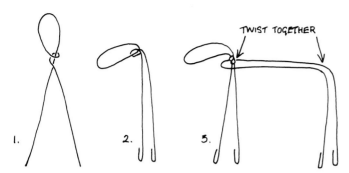

Fig 14: the wire framework for the dog

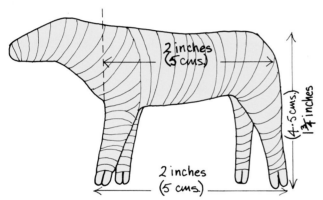

Fig 15: the dog after wrapping showing approximate measurements

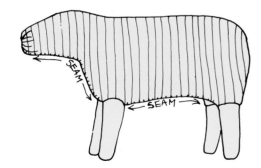

Fig 16: the dog with body cover in place

noting that each piece of wire is a *double* pipe-cleaner. Pad it lightly and bind this in place ready for the knitted cover (see Fig 15).

Begin at the nose, and cast on 12sts.

Rows 1–6; ss.

Rows 7–12; gt s.

Inc one st at beg of the next 6 rows (18sts).

K 6 rows straight.

Inc one st at beg of next 2 rows (20sts).

K 16 rows straight.

Last row; k 2 tog to end of row, thread the length of yarn on to a needle and draw this through the 10sts. This is the dog's tail-end. Gather the cast-on edge on to the dog's nose and sew up as in the diagram (Fig 16).

Legs

Cast on 6sts, k 12 rows. Gather last sts on to a thread for the foot-end. Pad and draw up; attach to body. Make 4.

Ears

In brown or tan yarn, cast on 4sts, k 4 rows.

Last row; k 2 tog twice, then cast off. Make 2.

Cow

This is worked in gt s all through, except for the horns and the udder. In this version, the legs are made separately from the body. You will need small amounts of 3 ply or 4 ply yarn in beige, or any other cow-colour you choose, also oddments of pink and brown. Size No13/2¼ mm and No11/3 mm needles and padding.

It will be found more convenient to attach the udder *before* the legs!

With size No11/3 mm needles, cast on 30sts and begin at the tail-end of the body. K 38 rows.

Row 39; k 2 tog, k 6, k 2 tog, k 10, k 2 tog, k 6, k 2 tog, (26sts).

Row 40; knit.

Row 41; dec one st at each end of row.

Repeat the last 2 rows until there are 18sts on the needle.

Row 48; k 12, turn and k 6. Work on the centre sts only – turn and k 5.

Turn and k 4.

Turn and k 2.

Turn and k 4.

Turn and k 6.

Turn and k to the end of the row.

Next row; dec one st at both ends of the row (16sts).

K 10 more rows.

Last row; k 2 tog to the end of the row, and gather these 8sts on to a thread and draw up.

Pad and close up the body.

The farmer tends his cows and the hens look for seeds.

Legs

Using size No13/2¼mm needles, cast on 12sts and work in gt s for 22 rows. Gather these sts on to a thread and draw up to form the foot, then sew up the seam, pad firmly and attach the cast-on edge to the body. Make 3 more in the same way. *Note:* the legs will look different from those in the photograph.

Ears

No13/2¼mm needles, cast on 5sts, work 8 rows of gt s.
Row 9; k 2 tog, k 1, k 2 tog.
Row 10; k 2 tog, k 1. Cast off. Fold in half and attach to the head as shown in the picture. Make 2.

Horns

Use paler yarn and No13/2¼mm needles, working in ss.
Cast on 6sts, work 10 rows, then k 2 tog 3 times.

Draw the 3 sts on to a thread and sew up. Pad slightly and attach as shown. Make 2.

Udder

Pink 3 ply yarn, No13/2¼mm needles, work in ss. 16sts, 6 rows.
Gather all sts on to a thread and draw up, pad and sew on.
Make 4 teats: 4sts, 4 rows of ss. Draw sts on to thread and sew on.

Tail

Using double yarn, make a crochet chain 2in/5cm long, and sew a tassel to the end. Fix this high up on the cow's back.
Embroider the markings on to the cow's body and the eyes and nose on to its face.

The skewbald pony in a field of flowers.

Pony

This is knitted all in one piece like a skin, beginning with the back legs and ending with the nose (Fig 17). It is a little more complicated than any of the other patterns, so if you prefer a simpler version it is suggested that you use the cow (body and legs) pattern, and substitute the pony's ears, mane and tail. You will need 3 ply or 4 ply yarns for the main body-colour and small oddments for the mane and tail. Padding will also be needed as well as needles size

No13/2¼ mm and No11/3 mm, and an extra pair. Garter st is used for all except the nose, and the hooves are made separately.

With the No11/3 mm needles, cast on 46sts and k 5 rows.

Next row; k 22, inc into next 2sts, k 22 (48sts).

Knit 7 more rows.

Row 14; k 23, inc into next 2sts, k 23 (50sts).

Row 15; k 8, turn and k 5 rows on these 8 sts with an

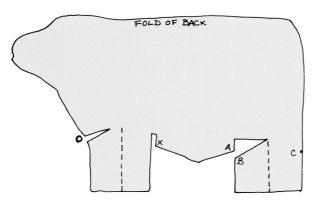

Fig 17: the shape of the pony skin

extra needle. Cast these 8 sts off and break off the yarn.

Rejoin the yarn to the centre section and k to the end of the row.

Row 17 as row 15.

Row 18; rejoin yarn to centre section and knit to end of row. Knit 3 rows on these 34sts

Row 22; cast on 3 sts, and k to end of row (37 sts).

Row 23; cast on 3 sts, and k to end of row (40 sts).

Row 24; inc into first st, k 18, k 2 tog, k 18, inc into last st (41 sts). Knit 7 more rows.

Row 32; k 2 tog, k 18, k 2 tog, k 17, k 2 tog (38 sts). Knit 6 more rows.

Rows 39 and 40; cast off 3 sts at beg of these 2 rows (32sts).

Rows 41 and 42; cast on 8 sts and k to end of row (48 sts).

Knit 10 rows on these 48 sts.

Row 53; k 8, turn and work 5 more rows on these 8 sts. Cast off.

Rejoin yarn to the centre section and k to end.

Row 55; as row 53. 32 sts remain.

Rejoin yarn to centre section, cast on 3 sts and k to end.

Row 57; cast on 3 sts and k to end (38 sts).

Shape neck

Next row; k 7, turn and k back on these 7 sts.

Next row; knit across all sts.

Repeat the last instructions 3 more times (i.e. twice at each side), then shape the top of the head.

Next row; k 23, turn, k 8, k to end.

Next row; knit across all sts.

Repeat this procedure twice more.

Shape nose

Next row; k 2 tog all along the row.

Now work 10 rows in ss.

Next row; k 1, k 2 tog all along the row, and gather the last sts on to a thread.

Ears

Use size No13/2¼ mm needles and work in ss. Cast on 7sts and work 5 rows. Then dec one st at each end of the 6th and 8th rows.

Draw the rem 3sts on to a thread and gather up. Make 2.

Hooves

Cast on 12sts in black yarn, and work 4 rows in gt s, then draw up all sts on to yarn and sew up to make a cup shape. Make 4.

Sew these on to the bottom of each leg.

Sew eyes and nostrils as shown, and cut lengths of contrasting yarn for the mane and tail.

Making up

Run a gathering thread around the cast-on-edge, then gather up to make a rounded tail-end. The padding of the 'pony-skin' is important to the success of the overall shape as it will tend to look very strange until the end of the process, when its eyes, ears, hooves mane and tail, have been added.

The diagram shows how to sew up the skin. Pad the legs before the body, and manipulate the padding gently to get a good shape, especially in the body around the neck.

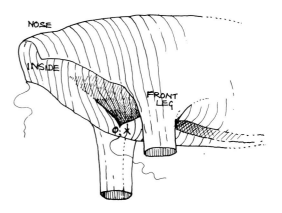

Fig 18: the front part of the pony showing the method of sewing the legs and under-seam

Donkey and mule

The basic shape is the same as that of the pony, but the donkey's mane and tail are different. See the photographs on pages 22 and 24. Also their ears are longer.

Rabbit

I have left the simplest one until last. It is made of a large white pom-pon body with two long knitted (or crocheted) ears. Tie a length of wool tightly around one side of the pom-pon to create the rabbit's head, then attach the ears.

The two children play with their rabbit.

ENCHANTED CASTLE

*The enchanted folk and animals
play happily beneath the castle walls,
while the brave knight
guards the little kingdom.*

CASTLE

This is the enchanted castle where the handsome prince lives with his brave knights. The exact height depends on the materials you have available, so the instructions given here are only general ones to illustrate how this model was made. It could easily become the container for all the small characters in this chapter, and would be a good project for a group of people to make.

You will need odd balls of grey and green DK yarn to cover the walls etc, and oddments of brown, orange and black yarns for the roof and details.
No10/3¼ mm, No9/3¾ mm and No8/4 mm needles.
You will also need pliable card for castle walls and roofs, and thick card for the bases. A large sheet of the former will be needed, as the walls are double thick-

The talking trees from the magic forest look on while the wicked witch sweeps the battlements with her broomstick.

ness, and the bases can be cut out of cardboard boxes. Toilet and kitchen roll tubes for turrets and towers. Glue and staples. Thick tapestry needles (for sewing), scissors, craft knife and pins.

Cardboard shape

For the base, draw round a dinner plate and cut 2 or 3 circles from 'box-card'. For the walls (see Fig 19), decide on the height of the tower and cut 2 strips of card to encircle the base, minus a gap of about 4 in/ 10 cm for the gateway. For extra strength, cut another piece to be stuck round the outside of the tower after the base and inside wall have been assembled. Fig 19 explains how these should be put together. Another narrow strip should be cut from spare card to go round the top edge as shown. Stick this in place and strengthen with staples too.

Cut two tall towers to go at each side of the gateway and make six small turrets as shown in Fig 19. Do not stick these in position yet.

Gateway towers

Use a fairly thick DK yarn and size No8/4 mm needles. Cast on 26sts and k 24 rows of gt s then change to ss and make reverse side the RS. Work 25 rows in rev ss. Begin the window: with RS facing, p 8, (k 1, p 1) for 10sts, p 8.

Next row; (WS) k 8, (p 1, k 1), for 10sts, k 8.

Next row; (RS) p 8, k 1, p 1, join in black yarn, k 6 in black, weaving in grey behind these 6 sts then in grey – k 1, p 1, p 8.

Next row; (WS) k 8, p 1, k 1, change to black p 6, change to grey, p 1, k 1, k 8.

Work these last 2 rows 5 more times (12 rows of window) the dec one black st at each side on every 2 rows, leaving off the moss st edges. Work 12 rows plain then make a set of small windows above as follows:

Next row; (RS) p 6, 2 black (4 grey, k 2 black) to last 6sts, p 6 grey.

Next row; k 6 grey, (p 2 black, k 4 grey) to last 8sts, k 2 black, k 6 grey.

Work 6 of these rows in all then change to grey to continue as before.

[Note: on the RS, on the first complete grey row above the windows, work 2 *knit* sts above the black sts of the previous row to avoid the colour change showing on the right side.]

Work 6 straight rows, then 10 rows of double moss st. Cast off in rib.

Sew up the 2 long sides and slip this on to the cardboard tube. Stick with glue at the top and bottom edges. Make 2.

Turrets

Using the same needles and yarn, cast on 24 sts and work in rev ss for 2 in/5 cm – about 14 rows – ending on a RS row (i.e. the rough side).

Cast on 2 sts and slide this piece on to the knob end of the needle. On the same needle, cast on another 12sts and work the same number of rows as the first piece. Push the two pieces together on the LH needle and work across both sets of sts, knitting through the back of the 2 cast-on sts and also on the next st. As you knit these 2 pieces together, weave the broken yarn in behind the knitting; this will not show on the RS. Work across these 26sts for 4 rows.

Now begin the windows as folls: break off 2 lengths of black yarn, each about 22 in/56 cm long and use these for the 2 separate windows to avoid tangling.

With WS facing (the smooth side) work as follows:

1st row; k 5 grey, y fwd, p 3 black, k 10 grey, y fwd, p 3 black, k 5 grey.

2nd row; p 5 grey, yarn to back and twist round black yarn, k 3 black, p 10 grey, yarn to back and twist round black yarn, k 3 black, p 5 grey.

Work 6 of these rows in all, remembering to twist the grey and black yarns at the beg of the 3 black sts to avoid making a hole.

Now work across all the sts in grey, but purl the 3sts above the windows (i.e. the black sts of the previous row) on the *first* row.

Work 4 grey rows and then cast off.

Sew up the edges from the top to within 2 in/5 cm of the lower edge, leaving the rest open to correspond with the slit in the centre of the knitting. Slip this on to the card tube, and align the 2 slits, then glue the knitting carefully in position so that no card shows. Glue round the top edge too. Make 6.

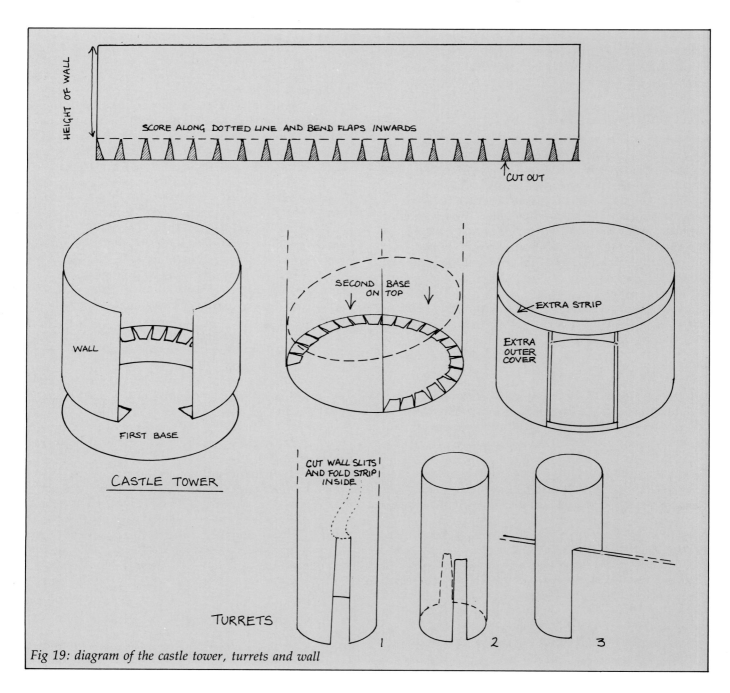

Fig 19: diagram of the castle tower, turrets and wall

Pointed roofs for towers and turrets

Make the 2 card roofs, (see Fig 20). Although they are slightly different, the same knitted cover is used for both sizes as it stretches to fit. Oddments of orange and brown 3–4 ply yarns are used and pieces of bendy card, staples and glue. Size No9/3½ or No10/3¼ mm needles. Changes in yarn and needle sizes will produce roofs of a different size too. You may also need a crochet hook.

Cast on 40sts and work 2 rows in ss.
Row 3; (k 2 tog, k 8) 4 times, (36sts).
Work three straight rows between each decrease row.
Row 7; (k 2 tog, k 7) 4 times, (32sts).
Row 11; (k 2 tog, k 6) 4 times, (28sts).
Row 15; (k 2 tog, k 2) 7 times, (21sts).
Row 19; (k 2 tog, k 1) 7 times, (14sts).
Row 23; (k 2 tog) 7 times.
Next row; p 7. Break off yarn, leaving a long end.
Gather the last sts on to the length of yarn and sew up to fit the card shape.

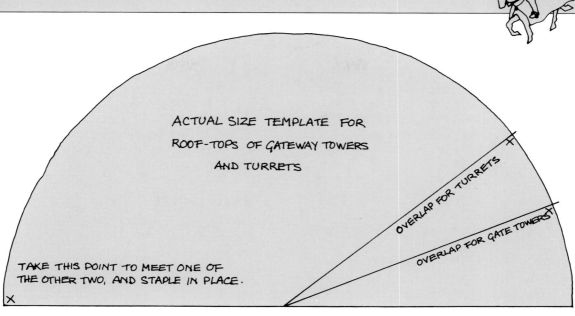

Fig 20: diagram of the crenellations and roof tops of the gateway towers and turrets

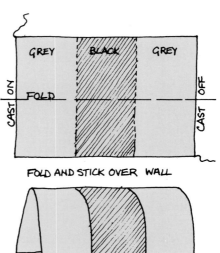

To neaten the edge, a tiny crochet st has been worked in to each knit st of the cast-on edge using a size No11/3 mm hook and a simple dc st, but this is optional. On the 2 gateway towers, another row of chained loops has been worked for extra decoration, but this is also optional.

Walls

To suit all measurements and shapes, and to make the knitting both easier and more interesting, the walls have been designed in separate strips going from top to bottom. These are then sewn together into one long piece, and the length can then be determined by the size of the tower you have made. If several people are working on this project, this would be an easy and painless way of covering a large surface, as long as the length of each piece (i.e. from the top of the wall to the base) was reasonably accurate. Any pieces which are a little too long can be folded over the top, and the width is not critical. The various textures/knitting stitches used will make the wall more interesting, even cables and lace patterns would be fun when combined with plain pieces. It could even be used as a sampler!

The pieces used on this castle are between 20 and 30 sts wide, using DK yarn on No8/4 mm needles, but there is no reason why different yarns cannot be used for this as long as the thicknesses are fairly similar. Use mossy green to suggest foliage too.

Crenellations

These are optional but add an authentic touch to the top of the castle walls, and are added as a series of long narrow strips after the walls have been covered with knitting and the turrets stuck in place on top of them. For the strip over the gateway, knit a narrow strip in rev ss to stretch from one gateway tower to the other – about 8–10 sts wide, with 10 rows in grey, 10 in black and 10 more in grey. The exact measurements will depend upon the individual castles. The small strips between the turrets are made separately (see Fig 20) and are glued on top of the knitted walls as shown.

Drawbridge

This is simply an oblong of card sandwiched between 2 pieces of knitting, one side in brown (any ridged pattern works well) and the other a paler colour/tone in smooth ss. The size of the card should be large enough to fit closely inside the gate area between the 2 towers, and the bottom edge can be sewn to the edge of the base. Measure the width of your gateway and be sure to cast on enough sts to cover the card piece. This drawbridge needed 32sts for a piece of card 5 in/13 cm wide, and a fancy rib st was used as follows.

Large eyelet rib

(you need a multiple of 6sts + 2 extra).
RS row 1; * p 2, k 4, * rep to last 2sts, p 2.
WS row 2; k 2, * p 4, k 2 *, rep from * to end.
Row 3; * p 2, k 2 tog, y fwd twice, s1 1, k 1, psso, * to last 2sts, p 2.
Row 4; k 2, * p 1, k into first y fwd and p into 2nd y fwd, p 1, k 2, rep from * to end.

Order of assembly

1. Stick knitted strip over gateway.
2. Cover walls, stick along top and bottom edges. Leave a narrow strip of card showing down each edge of the gateway.
3. Cover turrets and position on walls at equal distances.
4. With a fine skewer or thick needle, punch holes at ¼ in/1 cm intervals all the way down the bare strip of card at the sides of the gateway.
5. Cover the 2 gateway towers and sew these firmly in position through their knitted covers and into the holes of the card at each side of the gateway. Use a strong double thread (of yarn) for this, and a long needle.
6. If necessary, knit a strip to cover the *inside* of the narrow strip of card above the gateway.
7. Make the card roofs and knitted covers and stick these in place by gluing the top edges of the *towers*.
8. Make the crenellation strips to cover the top edges of the walls and stick these in place.
9. Make the drawbridge card and knitting, and fix in place.
10. For extra effect, you may wish to line the inside of the castle too, or even make a lid for it.

FIGURES AND ANIMALS

The basic framework for most of the enchanted characters is simple to make (see Fig 21). 3 ply yarn is used for all the clothes.

Basic body

1. Two pipe-cleaners are laid together and twisted as shown to make the head and arms.

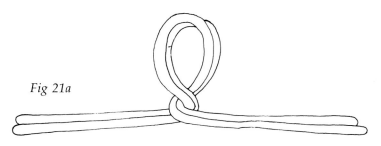

Fig 21a

2. Loop another pc, slip it over the head and twist it to make the top of the legs and body.

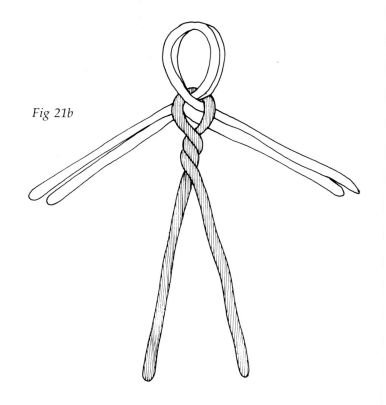

Fig 21b

Fig 21: making the wire frame body

3. Loop another pc in half and slip it over the head on the other side so that one loop lies to the front and the other to the back. Twist these and also the tops of the legs. Do a bit of pulling and tugging at this stage to ensure that the arms do not get pushed too far down the frame and look as if they come from the middle of the body.

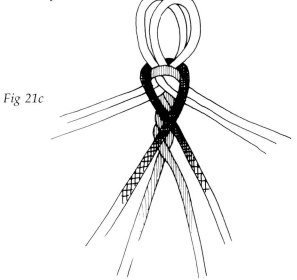

Fig 21c

4. Make two legs as follows: one pc bent double, bend up about ½ in/1 cm at the folded end to form the foot. Lay this leg-section alongside the leg which is attached to the body, so that the overall height measures no more than 4½ in/11 cm. Bind the 2 leg pieces together with sticky tape. Turn up the arms to make them equal length.

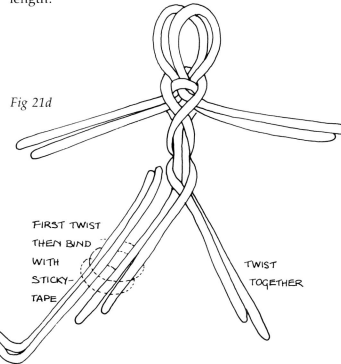

Fig 21d

FIRST TWIST
THEN BIND
WITH
STICKY-
TAPE

TWIST
TOGETHER

5. Bind the head, body and arms with thick pink yarn, sewing the ends into the body and wrapping around the neck tightly as shown.

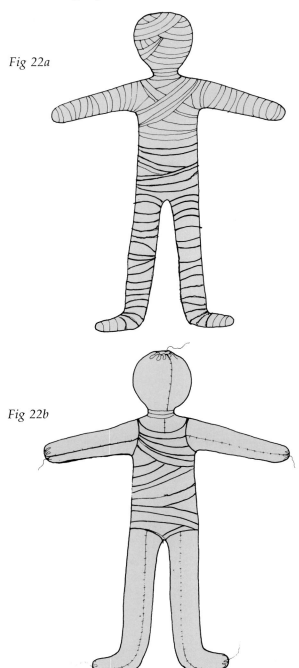

Fig 22a

Fig 22b

Fig 22: wrapping the body and the knitted covering

KNITTED BODY COVERING

Begin with the head and knit in ss throughout. Use 2 ply baby yarn and size No15/1½ mm needles, or finer. You will need about 20sts for the head covering, and about 18 rows to make a piece which continues down past the neck and well on to the shoulders. Gather the last sts on to a thread and draw these up to form the top of the head as shown. Sew the seam up the back and run a tight gathering thread around the neck. Sew the cast-on edge to the shoulder area.

Legs

Make legs on about 10sts as long as necessary for each figure to the top of the leg. Draw the last sts up on to a length of yarn and gather. Sew up the seam, and sew on to the complete body.

Arms

For the arms, you will need about 10sts. As with the legs, the pieces are not cast off but gathered up at the ends of the limbs. Attach the arm pieces well up on to the shoulder covering.

Prince

The handsome and charming prince of all the best stories wears eighteenth-century style dress, tight breeches tucked into tall riding boots, a fitted jacket edged with gold, the lace cuffs and cravat show at wrists and neck, and on his natural brown curls, (tied back with ribbon), he wears a three-cornered hat from which hangs a plume of feathers. The shirt, to make less bulk under the jacket, takes the form of a vest-front, so the lace cuffs are added to the sleeves of his jacket.

BREECHES AND BOOTS

These are made all in one piece. Beginning at the waist and using 3 ply deep yellow yarn and No14/2mm needles, cast on 10sts and work in ss for 25 rows. On the next row, dec one st at each end to make 8sts. Change to brown 3 ply for boots, and continue in ss for 18 rows, or until long enough to reach the end of the foot. Draw the sts up on to a threaded needle and sew up as far as the top of the boot. Make another piece the same. Sew centre back and centre front seams, slip on to the body, putting the feet into the boots, and sew down the legs. The boots may have a gold band embroidered round the tops. Darn all ends in.

SHIRT FRONT AND CRAVAT

This is simply an oblong of ss. Cast on 10sts and work 13 rows using fine white 3 ply. On the 14th row; knit. 15th row; purl. 16th row; knit, then cast off p-wise. These last rows form the neck edge. Sew this piece to the front of the body to slightly overlap the top of the breeches.

For the cravat, make 2 separate pieces and sew the narrow edges to the neckband of the shirt. Cast on 8sts and work in single rib for 5 rows.
Next row; (k 2 tog) 4 times.
Next row; k.
Next row; p, then cast off k-wise.
The second piece is the same except that the last 2 rows are omitted. This piece is sewn on top of the other.

COAT

Begin at the lower edge, and with No 14/2mm needles and deep yellow 3 ply yarn, cast on 22sts and work in single rib for 10 rows.
Next row; (k 2 tog, k 8) twice, k 2 tog.
Next row; p.
Next row; k 2 tog, k 6, k 2 tog, k 7, k 2 tog, (16sts).
Next row; p.
Continue in ss until the underarm division for the sleeves, (i.e. about 4 more rows).
Next row; work on the first 4sts for 7 rows.
Break off yarn and rejoin it to the centre 8sts. Work 7 rows. Break yarn and rejoin to the last 4sts and work 7 rows, then p across all 16sts. P one more row, k the next and cast off p-wise.
With gold metallic yarn, work an edge of crochet, using a No12/2.50mm crochet hook, all the way round the coat beginning at the centre of the back edge.

Sleeves

Cast on 10sts and work 8 rows in ss.
9th row; p, then break off yarn and change to white (as for shirt).
10th row; p, and cast off p-wise.
This makes a tiny white cuff on to which the lace ruffle is crocheted, so do not break the yarn, but using a No12/2.50 mm hook, crochet a frill along this edge as follows:
Next row; *3 ch, 1 dc into next ch sp * to end.

You may knit this frill if you prefer

Darn in unwanted ends at this stage and sew the lace cuff with rem white yarn. Sew up the rest of the sleeve and slide it on to the arm, placing the seam at the back. With metallic yarn, embroider a whip stitch over the p row along the cuff edge. Sew the sleeve to the coat armhole. Make 2.

HAIR AND FACE

Using mottled brown yarn and the same needles, cast on 14sts and work in gt s for 10 rows. Over the next 4 rows, k 2 tog at each end to make 6sts, (i.e. on alt rows).
Work in single rib for 8 rows on these 6sts , then cast off in rib. Gather the cast-on edge with a running st and sew up to form the crown of the head. Embroider the face, and then sew the hair on to the head. Make a

*The handsome prince carries the princess away
on his white horse and they live happily ever after.*

ribbon of crochet chain and tie this round the bunch of hair at the nape of the neck.

THREE-CORNERED HAT

For the crown of the hat, cast on 14sts and work 4 rows ss. Gather the last row and sew up the seam.

For the brim, cast on 16sts and work 2 rows in ss then *k 1, inc in next st, repeat from * to the end of the row, (24sts).

Next row; p.

Next row; * k 1, inc in next st, repeat from * to the end of the row, (36sts).

Next row; p.

Last row; k, then cast off p-wise and sew up the 2 short edges.

Sew the cast-on edge of the brim to cast-on edge of the crown, then fold up the brim to make 3 points at equal distances. Sew to the crown in the centre of each side (do not sew right along to the point, but run the needle through the crown to the centre of each side) with a few firm sts. Sew the hat to the head with one point at the front. The feathers are made from a crochet chain about 4 in/10 cm long, sewn into a bunch. Fluffy yarn is best for this.

Princess

The princess can be made to match your own individual ideas of what an enchanting princess should look like, colour of hair, clothes, and so on. Our princess wears a circlet of (crochet chain) glittery yarn over her auburn shoulder length hair, a deep blue embroidered gown (actually the pattern is knitted in) over an underskirt of white lace. The frilly white collar and sleeves ruffles, and the sparkling slippers complete the outfit, (see page 45).

You will need size No13/2¼ mm needles and a No12/2.50 mm crochet hook; 3 ply blue and white, a glittery yarn for the circlet, and a blue metallic yarn for the skirt pattern, and slippers. Brown (auburn) yarn for hair and oddments for features.

SKIRT

If the underskirt appears to be too 'holey' you may have to make another white layer beneath as I have done. This is simply an oblong gathered at the waist.

White underskirt and vest

The vest is a tiny oblong of rev ss, (8sts, 5 rows), sewn across the front of the body.

For the underskirt, cast on 50sts and work about 30 rows altogether, but to obtain the lacy effect, make half

of this amount in picot st or any other simple lacy st. (Picot st is made on 2 rows: * k 2 tog, y fwd repeat from * to end of row, then p the next row. This makes a row of holes).

The next-to-the-last row of the skirt should be decreased as follows; k 2 tog all across the row to make 25sts, then p the last row and cast off. Join the 2 side edges, gather the top, fit on to the waist, and sew in place.

Blue divided overskirt

Cast on 70sts in blue yarn (A) and use metallic blue yarn as the secondary colour (B). [Note: for a simpler version, use plain ss.]

Rows 1 & 2; use colour B and k 2 rows.

Row 3; A, (k 4, sl 2) to the last 4 sts, k 4.

Row 4; A, (p 4, sl 2 p-wise) to the last 4 sts, p 4.

Rows 5 & 6; as rows 3 & 4.

Rows 7 & 8; B, k all sts.

Row 9; A, k 1, (sl 2, k 4) to last 3 sts, sl 2, k 1.

Row 10; A, p 1, (sl 2 p-wise, P 4) to last 3 sts, sl 2, p 1.

Rows 11 & 12; as rows 9 & 10.

Repeat these 12 rows once more, then rows 1 & 2 again. Work 2 rows in A (ss).

Continue working in ss and dec on the k rows as follows:

Next row; (k 5, k 2 tog) 10 times.

Next and alt rows; p.

Next row; (k 2 tog, k 4) 10 times, (50sts).

Continue in ss on these sts until the waistline is reached, then k 2 tog all along the row (25 sts), then p one row. Cast off. Press the bottom edge *very gently* under a damp cloth to prevent it rolling up.

BODICE

Begin at the lower back (see Fig 23), cast on 9 sts and work in ss for 8 rows.

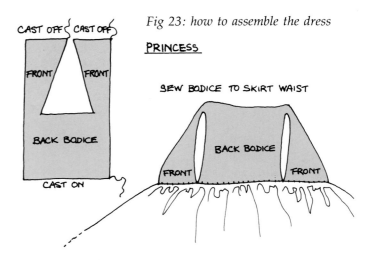

Fig 23: how to assemble the dress

SLIP THE BODICE AND SKIRT ON TO THE FIGURE AND STITCH THE TWO FRONT EDGES ONTO THE WHITE VEST.

9th row; k 2, cast off 5, k 2.

Work on the 2 sets of 2sts for 3 rows, then inc one st on the inside edge (i.e. the neck edge) on *alternate* rows until there are 5sts on each side. P one more row and cast off.

Making up

Gather the skirt waistband to fit the figure closely, leaving a gap of about ¼in/6 mm at the front. Do not sew on to the figure at this stage. Now follow the instructions on the diagram.

Sleeves

With blue yarn, cast on 20sts and work in ss for 4 rows.

5th row; k 2 tog across all sts to make 10sts.

6th row; p.

Change to blue metallic yarn, k one row and cast off k-wise.

Sew up the side seam and gather the top edge to fit the armhole. Sew this in place on to the bodice, pushing the sleeve edge up on to the 'elbow'. Now make a lace cuff as follows: with the fine white yarn, cast on 24sts and k 2 rows, then k 2 tog across all sts to make 12. Cast off.

Gather the cast off edge, sew up the side edges, and then stitch the lace cuff to the sleeve edge. Make 2.

Lace collar

With the same yarn as the cuffs, cast on 40sts and k 2 rows. Picot st for 2 rows.

Next row; p 2 tog across all sts to make 20sts and cast off k-wise.

Sew cast-off edge to dress, (see Fig 23).

SHOES

Use blue metallic yarn, cast on 8sts and work in ss until long enough to slip over the foot (about 10 rows). Sew up the heel and gather the last row on to a thread and draw up over the toe. Sew this on to the foot.

HAIR AND FACE

Using brown (auburn) yarn for hair, cast on 16sts and work 4 rows in gt s.

5th row; p.

6th row; (k 2 tog, k 5) twice, k 2 tog, (13sts).

Work the next 13 rows in ss then gather all sts tog on a thread and draw up. Stitch this part to the top of the head, sew down the edges to the face and along the nape of the neck above the gt s edge.

Embroider the face.

The tiara, or circlet, is a crochet chain of glittery yarn made into a circle and stitched to the hair.

Knight

As the entire body is encased in shining armour, only the face requires a pink cover with embroidered eyes. For this, use a fine 2 ply dark flesh-coloured yarn on size No14/2 mm needles, and work on 22sts for 14 rows. Gather the last sts for the top of the head. The colour used on the cloak, shield and plume should all be the same, and if he rides on horseback, the trappings and harness should also be the same. The suit of armour is made from two main pieces; the helmet and tunic all-in-one, and the trousers and feet together. Any metallic colour will look good, gold, silver or bluish-silver. The helmet has another piece added on top of the 'hood' to give height, and this has a band of gold thread worked in. Measurements should be checked at all stages as yarns differ, see photo on page 48.

You will need size No14/2 mm and No15/1½ mm needles; metallic yarn, small amounts of contrasting coloured 3 ply for cloak, plume, and eyes; a small piece of thick card and one paper-stud for the shield. For the banner you will need a small lollipop stick and gold paper.

TROUSERS

These begin at the toe end. With metallic yarn and size No14/2 mm needles, cast on 10sts and work in ss for 24 rows, then inc one st at each end of next row (12sts). Work 25 more rows and cast off. Make another piece the same.

Sew these 2 pieces together from the top as far as the top of the legs, slip this part on to the body and pin at the waist. Gather the 2 cast-on edges at the feet, and sew up the leg seams (with the legs inside). Stitch the waist edge to the body.

TUNIC AND UNDER-HELMET

These begin at the lower edge of the front. Use the same yarn and needles, and * cast on 14sts and work 2 rows in ss. Work 2 rows of gold thread, then change back to silver for 2 rows. Dec one st at each end of the next row * and work 21 more rows, without shaping. (12sts.)

For the face-opening, k 3, cast off 6, k 3.

Work on the first set of 3 sts for 7 rows in ss, break the yarn and connect to the other 3 sts and work 6 rows on these.

Next row; turn, cast on 5sts, k across the other 3sts, (11sts).

Next row; p across the complete row, working into the back of the 9th st. Work 2 more rows, gather sts on to a thread and draw up.

For the back, work as for the front from * to *, then work 36 more rows, without shaping. Gather sts on to

The brave knight in silver armour and his horse are ready for battle.

a thread and draw up. Sew these 2 pieces tog from the lower edges, leaving a space for the arms. Slip this on to the body, sew the shoulders and round the neck and on up to the under-helmet. Sew the face-opening round the face.

Sleeve and hand
This is made all in one piece.
Cast on 20sts and work 22 rows in ss.
Do not cast off, gather the sts on to a thread and fit this part on to the hands. Stitch up the sleeve seam and attach the tops to the armhole of the tunic. Make another in the same way.

HELMET

The extra helmet fits over the top of the other and pulls well down over the forehead. Cast on 22sts and work in gt s for 7 rows, the 3rd and 4th of these being in gold thread.
8th row; p.
Gather all sts on to a thread and sew up the sides.
The plume is a thick, short tassel in the colours chosen for the other accessories. Sew it firmly to the top of the helmet and use a dab of glue to hold it in place at the back.

CLOAK

Gold 3 ply yarn was used for this but any other yarn will do as long as the measurements are checked against the figure. Using No15/1½ mm needles, cast on 12 sts and work 20 rows in ss. At this point, introduce bands of colour (6 rows were used on the model) and on the last of these rows, 3 extra sts were made, one at each end and one in the centre (15sts). Work 4 more rows and cast off. Sew the top edge round the neck.

SHIELD

This is a tiny shaped piece of gold card on to which has been glued a crocheted circle of gold yarn. It is fastened to the knight's left arm with a paper stud which passes through the centre of the circle and curves round on to the arm behind.

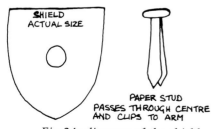

Fig 24: diagram of the shield

BANNER

Paint the lollipop stick silver. Cut a length of gold paper, fold and glue wrong sides together around the top of the pole, then cut out the banner shape.

Horse

It is quite important to spend time on the horse's framework, as this is the largest of our animals and must take the weight of a knight in full armour! (See page 50). Use plenty of pcs (allow 16 to 20), pad him carefully and wrap very firmly with yarn before making the cover. Remember that the cover adds something to the height and bulk of the horse. Aim for an upright stance, long slender legs and a not-too-fat body.

The padding should begin at the head-end: gently bandage the wire frame with long narrow strips of padding, making it bulkier around the shoulders, chest and hindquarters. Do not pad the legs except for the tops, but use the wrapping/binding yarn to separate the hindquarters under the tail. The legs should be wrapped with yarn to make them strong and smooth, but should remain slender.

The trappings worn during jousting were more for identification purposes than anything else as the colours and designs matched those of the rider, but for us, they serve the dual purpose of hiding a less-than-perfect model. They are, of course, optional, and can be made in any colour and design you choose. You may find that a row-counter would be useful.

You will need the following needles: No15/1½ mm, No13/2¼ mm, No12/2¾ mm and No11/3 mm, and a small crochet hook; 1oz/25 gm ball of 4 ply in main body-colour, small amounts for the mane and tail, and a bright colour for the trappings and harness and white yarn for the saddle (4 ply); blue and yellow 4 ply for the horse's coat; black yarn for the hooves; one gold or silver button to decorate the horse's coat.

KNITTED COVER

The forelegs and underbody gusset are made in 3 separate pieces; the back legs and body are made in 2 separate pieces which are then joined so that the head and neck are a continuation of these, (see Fig 26).

Forelegs
Use No12/2¾ mm needles and begin with black yarn for the hooves, cast on 8sts and work 4 rows in ss. Change to body colour and inc one st at both ends of next row, (10sts). Work 13 more rows, then inc again as before, and again on the 23rd row, (14sts).
P one more row and then cast off 2sts at beg of next 2 rows. Dec one st at both ends of next and every foll k row until only 2sts rem. Cast off. Make 2.
Sew the legs up and slip them on to the framework with the points to the outside and the seams inside.

Right back leg
* Cast on 8sts with black yarn and work 4 rows in ss.

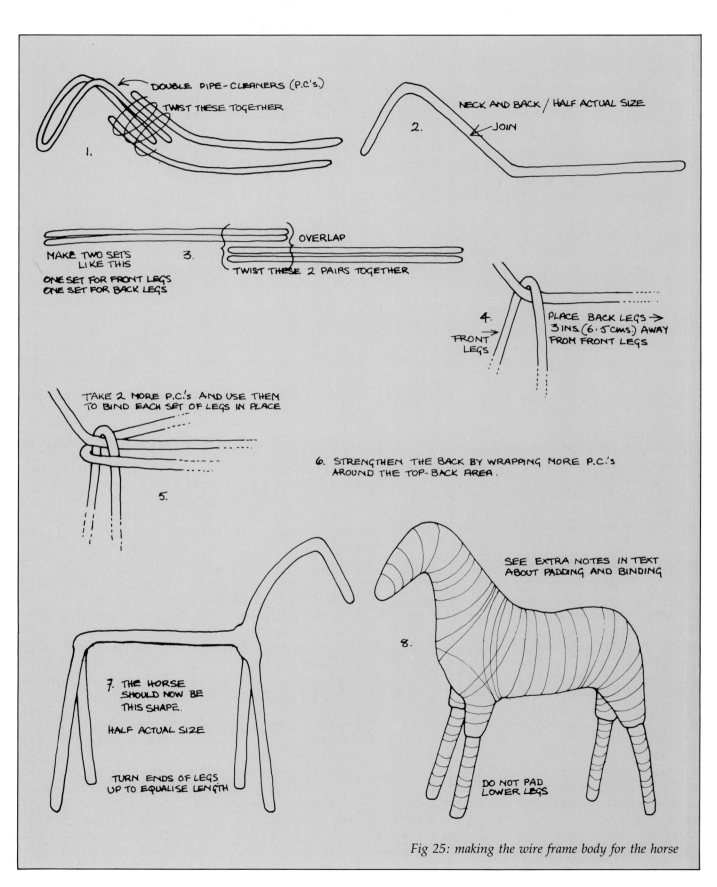

1. DOUBLE PIPE-CLEANERS (P.C.'s)

TWIST THESE TOGETHER

2. NECK AND BACK / HALF ACTUAL SIZE

JOIN

3. OVERLAP

MAKE TWO SETS LIKE THIS

TWIST THESE 2 PAIRS TOGETHER

ONE SET FOR FRONT LEGS
ONE SET FOR BACK LEGS

4. FRONT LEGS

PLACE BACK LEGS →
3 INS (6.5 CMS.) AWAY
FROM FRONT LEGS

5. TAKE 2 MORE P.C.'s AND USE THEM
TO BIND EACH SET OF LEGS IN PLACE

6. STRENGTHEN THE BACK BY WRAPPING MORE P.C.'s
AROUND THE TOP-BACK AREA.

7. THE HORSE
SHOULD NOW BE
THIS SHAPE.

HALF ACTUAL SIZE

TURN ENDS OF LEGS
UP TO EQUALISE LENGTH

8. SEE EXTRA NOTES IN TEXT
ABOUT PADDING AND BINDING

DO NOT PAD
LOWER LEGS

Fig 25: *making the wire frame body for the horse*

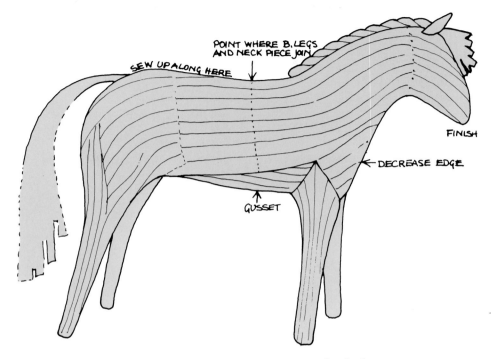

Fig 26: assembling the knitted cover for the horse

Change to body-colour and inc one st at both ends of next row; (10sts).

Work 9 more rows (14 in all).

15th row; inc one st at each end of row, also on 19th, 21st and 23rd rows, (18sts). Purl alt rows.

25th row; inc in 1st st, k 8, M 1, k 8, inc in last st.

26th row; p.

27th row; inc, k 9, M 1, K 10, inc.

28th row; p, (24sts) *.

At this point, you can add extra rows to make the legs longer if you need to. You should have reached the top of the leg.

Next row; cast off 5sts, k to end.

Next row; cast off 3sts, p to end.

Next row; (k 3, inc in next st) 3 times, k 4.

Next row; p.

Next row; (k 4, inc in next st) 3 times, k 4.

Next row; p.

Next row; (k 5, inc) 3 times, k 4.

Next row; p.

Next row; (k 6, inc) 3 times, k 4, (28sts).

Begin shaping to turn on to the back:

Next row; p 2 tog, p across rest of sts until you reach the last st. Leave this on the LH needle, turn, and k back.

Repeat this procedure, leaving one extra st on the LH needle at the end of every p row (remembering to p 2 tog at the beginning) until 11sts rem unworked on the LH side and 6 'worker' sts on the RH side, (17sts in all). Turn and k back, then p across all sts. Continue without shaping for 8 more rows.

Next row; k 12, turn and p back.

Next row; k 7, turn and p back.

Next row; k 2, turn and p back.

Work 2 complete rows across all these sts and then leave them on a spare needle until the left leg has been made.

Left back leg

Work as for right leg from * to *.

Next row; cast off 3 sts at beg of row, k to end.

Next row; cast off 5 sts at beg of row, p to end.

Next row; k 4 (inc in next st, k 3) 3 times. Purl alternate rows.

Next row; k 4 (inc, k 4) 3 times.

Next row; k 4 (inc, k 5) 3 times.

Next row; k 4 (inc, k 6) 3 times, (28sts).

Now begin the back shaping as follows:

Next row; k 2 tog, k to last st, leave this on LH needle, turn and p back.

Repeat these 2 rows, leaving one extra st on the LH needle at the end of every k row (remembering to k 2 tog at the beg) until 11sts rem unworked on the LH needle and 6 'workers' on the RH side, (17 sts in all). Turn and p back. Continue without shaping for 7 more rows.

Next row; p to last 2sts, turn and k back.

51

Next row; p to last 7sts, turn and k back.
Next row; p to last 12sts, turn and k back.
Work 3 complete rows leaving the sts on the needle.

Neck and head

Slip both sets of sts on to the same needle, back to back, and join them together by sewing (on the wrong side) along the back, from the needle to the 3 cast off sts. With the RS facing, cast on 10sts, k 2 tog on the centre 2 sts, k to end.
Next row; cast on 10sts and p to end.
Next row; k 2 tog, k to centre 2 sts and k these tog, k to last 2 sts, k 2 tog.
Next row; p.
Repeat the last 2 rows until there are 29sts.
Next row; k 2 tog at each end of row only.
Next row; p.
Repeat these last 2 rows once more, (25sts).
Next row; k 24, leave one st on LH needle, turn and p 23, leaving one st on LH needle. Turn, k to last 2sts, (leave 2 on LH needle) turn, p back to last 2 sts, and leave these on LH needle.
Continue in this way, leaving one extra st on LH needle at the end of every row until there are 8 unworked sts at each side of the row.
Turn and knit back on 17sts then p a complete row on 25sts.
Work 4 rows straight, then dec one st at each end of next row and continue without shaping on 23sts for 5 more rows.
Next row; k 2 tog, k 8, sl 1, k 2 tog, psso, k 8, k 2 tog.
Next row; p 19.
Next row; k 2 tog, k 15, k 2 tog.
Next row; p 17.
Next row; k 2 tog, k 5, sl 1, k 2 tog, psso, k 5, k 2 tog.
Next row; p 13.
Next row; (k 2 tog) 6 times, k 1.
Gather these last sts over the nose.

Gusset

Make this after the rest of the coverings have been fitted.
Important note: the exact size of this is important to the fit of the 'skin cover' and so the number of sts and rows must be adjusted according to the size of the gap left underneath the body. Watch for these * marks and make your adjustments where they occur.
Begin at the chest end and cast on 2sts and work 2 rows.
Now inc one st at both ends of every k row until there are * 8sts, (or less).
Purl one row. Cast on * 8 (or less) sts at beg of the next 2 rows.
Work 2 rows straight, then dec each side as folls:
Next row; k 1, sl 1, k 1, psso, k to last 3 sts, k 2 tog, k 1.

Next row; p.
Repeat these 2 rows until * 6sts rem.
Continue without shaping (if necessary) until long enough and cast off.

Making up

Pin the gusset in place (with the cast off edge at the rear) and sew to the tops of the forelegs.
Sew up the seams of the back legs and slip these on to the frame, pulling the head piece over the head and drawing up the gathering thread at the nose end. Pin all round on to the gusset and sew up with yarn and an invisible st.

Ears

Use No15/1½ mm needles, cast on 6 sts and work in ss for 6 rows.
Next row; k 2 tog, k 2, k 2 tog.
Next row; p.
Next row; (k 2 tog) twice.
Cast off, fold in half lengthwise and sew on to the head. Make 2.

Tail

This is a long tassel which has been bound round the top part for 1 in/2.5 cm to shape it. Fix it high up on to the horse's back end as shown, and trim so that the tassel is shorter on the underside.

Mane

Make a very thick plait long enough to reach from the base of the neck to well over the forehead. Tie it off between the ears, leaving ends of about 1 in/2 cm hanging free to form the forelock. Sew this in place with firm back sts.

OTHER DETAILS

The white blaze can be made by knitting a small oblong of white yarn and sewing it down the centre of the face. White socks can also be made in this way and sewn on afterwards. The eyes are large and dark: sew them well up on the head as shown.

HARNESS AND TRAPPINGS

The bridle and reins are made of short lengths of crochet chain, and a length of knitted cast-on and cast-off stitches. These short lengths are then sewn together and on to the horse's head. The blue decoration on the reins are small oblongs of gt s made on 20sts and 6 rows (size No14/2 mm needles) and these are then sewn on to the reins.

Brown horse's blue and yellow coat

Using 4 ply yarn and No10/3¼ mm needles, work from the chart on page 54. The white saddle is knitted into the coat, and has been outlined with a line of yellow chain st.
The little stirrups to keep the knight's feet in place are simply chained loops which are sewn firmly into the

The white horse is saddled and bridled and waits patiently for the prince.

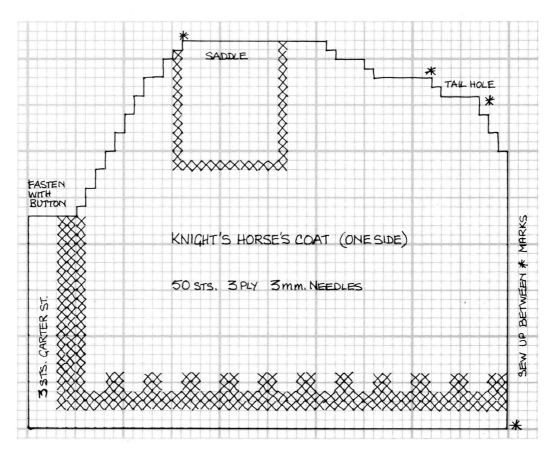

In the diagram:
- SADDLE
- TAIL HOLE
- FASTEN WITH BUTTON
- 3 STS. GARTER ST.
- KNIGHT'S HORSE'S COAT (ONE SIDE)
- 50 STS. 3 PLY 3 mm. NEEDLES
- SEW UP BETWEEN * MARKS

Fig 27: diagram for the horse's coat

corners of the saddle patch on the horse's coat.
The horse's coat is made in two pieces which are then sewn together along the top edges. Sew down the back edges from * to * leaving the rest open for the tail. You may need to gather this hole up with a running thread to fit on to the back. Leave the front edges open, and fasten at the neck with a gold or silver button for decoration.

White horse's saddle
Use 4 ply yarn and size No13/2¼ mm needles.
Cast on 8sts and work in gt s. Work 1 row, then inc one st at each end of 2nd row, knit the 3rd row, and on the 4th row inc again as on the 2nd, (12sts).
Work straight for 3 in/7.5 cm from the beg.
Dec one st at each end of next 2 alt rows, (8sts), then cast off 2sts at beg of next 2 rows. Continue on the rem 4sts for the girth, until this is long enough to pass under the body to the other side of the saddle. Make the stirrups as for the blue and yellow coat.

Witch and black cat

Traditionally, witches appear in black and sombre colours, but our version is more colourful and wears a very dark purple over-dress which has lighter cuffs and border, and under this she wears a multiple coloured skirt over dark leg coverings. Make her leg coverings first, at the same time as her face and hand covers. Then embroider her face (not too pretty) and knit her grey hair, as this helps to give her a certain character before you make her clothes. Keep her wrapped up warm while you're doing this, as witches get cross easily!
You will need No14/2 mm and No13/2¼ mm needles; small amounts of dark purple 3 ply (or dark grey) for the over-dress and random-dyed yarn for the under-skirt. Also small amounts of mid-purple and dark yarn for the dress and legs. Grey 3 ply for the hair and black for the hat. Oddments of yarns for the features.
The cat is made in rev ss in dark charcoal, 3 ply, and a

The wicked witch and her cat cast spells under
the pom-pon bush in the magic forest.

tiny amount of green will be needed for the eyes and white for the whiskers.

For the broomstick you will need oddments of brown yarn and thin wire.

HAIR AND HAT
This is knitted all in one piece.
Begin with the hair; using grey yarn and No13/2¼ mm needles, cast on 22sts and work in single rib for 12 rows.

Row 13; k 2 tog all along the row, (11sts).
Row 14; change to black yarn and p one row.
Continue in ss as follows for the top of the hat: work 6 rows straight, then (k 2 tog, k 1) to last 2sts, k 2 tog. Work 3 rows straight, then (k 2 tog) 3 times to last st, k1. P one row, then (k 2 tog) twice. Cast off.

Sew up the black point, leaving the grey hair open to frame the face. Now make the brim as follows: with black yarn, cast on 30sts and k 3 rows.
Next row; (k 1, k 2 tog) 10 times, then k one more row.
Next row; (k 2 tog, k 3) 4 times. Cast off loosely.
Sew up the 2 short sides to form a circle. Stitch the hair on to the witch's head, pulling it well down, then slip the brim over and sew, making sure that no grey hair shows on top.

SKIRT

In random-dyed 3 ply yarn and with size No13/2¼ mm needles, cast on 30sts and work 3 rows in gt s. Change to ss and work 25 more rows, or until long enough to reach from waist to mid-calf, (i.e. not quite full-length).
Next row; (k 1, k 2 tog) 10 times.
Cast off p-wise. Sew up the back seam, gather the top edge and sew round the waist.

OVER-DRESS

Using the same needles and mid-purple yarn, cast on 36sts and work 4 rows in gt s (beginning at the lower edge), then continue in ss for 6 more rows. (If you wish, introduce a few rows of rev ss among these 6.) In the next k row, change to dark-purple yarn, and work 2 more rows.
Next row; k 2 tog to the end of the row, (18sts), then work 11 more rows in ss.
Divide the sts into sets of 5, 8, and 5sts for the armholes. Work on these sets of sts separately for 9 rows each. Work a k row across all sts and then cast off.
Fit this on to the body and sew up the back seam.

Sleeves

Use mid-purple for the cuffs and cast on 10sts. Work 2 rows in gt s then change to dark-purple and work 9 rows in ss. Cast off. Make 2. Sew up the side seams, slip the sleeves on to the arms and sew the dress around the armholes.

BROOM

2 pcs twisted tightly together will make the broom handle. Bend the doubled ends over top and bottom and wrap tightly with brown yarn. Tie together a bundle of trimmed thin wire and attach to one end of the handle with a length of brown yarn.

CAT

The diagram above shows the pc frame used for the cat. You will need about 4 pcs and the frame should be slightly padded and wrapped to give the shape.

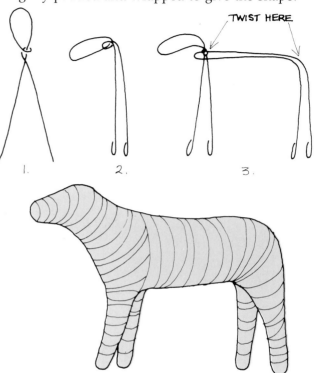

Fig 28: making the wire frame and padding the body of the cat

Using dark charcoal yarn and No14/2 mm needles cast on 10sts and work in rev ss for 6 rows. Cast on 4sts at the beg of next row and work straight for 8 rows. Cast off 4sts at the beg of next row and work straight for 6 rows. Cast off.
Slip the knitted cover over the padded body; sew over the head first, and run a thread around the neck to gather in. Stitch down the chest and gather a thread round the back edge to fit over the hindquarters as far as the legs.
Now make 4 legs: on 5sts, work in rev ss for about 10 rows (measure for exact size). Now sew these up and attach to the top of the cat's body.
The ears can be embroidered more easily than knitted. Use double yarn and make two or three sts leaving a tiny loop with each one, then take several sts into these loops, over and over, until large enough. Make the tail from a crochet chain using a fine hook and 3 strands of yarn. Embroider the eyes in green and sew on some long white whiskers.

Wizard

True to tradition, the wizard must *look* magical, and so he wears a long gown of bright colours and a tall pointed cap, though magicians do vary and you may have other ideas. His skin shows only on face and hands, as his legs and feet are covered in brown. The overgown takes the form of a long waistcoat, as the sleeves of this outer garment and those of the under-gown are knitted in one piece. The overgown is split up the sides as far as the armholes.

You will need No14/2 mm and No13/2¼ mm needles;

The wizard rests under the shade of a blossom tree as he journeys through the magic forest.

small amounts of 3 ply turquoise for the undergown, and 3 ply random-dyed yarn for the overgown. If you cannot obtain this, try using a plain 3 ply together with a fine glittery yarn, but check the measurements as you go along. Red 3 ply was used for the hat (a very small amount), brown 3 ply for the legs and feet, metallic yarn for the buckle, white 2 ply for the hair and beard, and oddments for the features. 3 ply white yarn with a glitter thread running through it was used for the staff.

You will also need a large pretty sequin, or bead, for the jewel in the hat and some glue. You may like him to wear a heavy chain and jewel around his neck, or dress him in black and cover him in sparkling sequins.

OVERGOWN

Use No13/2¼ mm needles and random-dyed yarn; begin at the back and cast on 18sts. Work 32 rows in ss, then cast off 3sts at beg of next 2 rows. Dec one st at each end of foll 2 k rows, (8sts). Work 5 more rows and leave these 8sts on a pin.

For the left front, cast on 9sts and work in ss for 32 rows but k the last 2 sts of every row. Cast off 3 sts at beg of 33rd row. Dec one st at beg of next 2 k rows. Work 6 more rows then leave these 4sts on a pin.

For the right front, use the same instructions as for the left front *except* that the first 2sts of every row should be knitted. Reverse the armhole shaping. Place all three pieces back on to the needle (in the right order, armhole to armhole) and k across all sts. (in gt s) for 4 rows, dec at both ends of the last row, then cast off.

Sleeves

Darn all ends in, then with RS facing and random-yarn, pick up 22sts around the armhole and work 4 rows in ss and 2 rows in rev ss. Chage to the same colour yarn as the undergown and p 2 tog all along the row, (11sts). Work in ss to the wrist, about 3 rows, then cast off. Make 2.

Darn ends in and press gently, sew up the lower sleeve edge and then the overgown sleeves, leaving about 2 in/5 cm open up the sides of the gown.

UNDERGOWN

Cast on 16sts and work 24 rows in ss. You may wish to insert a few rows of moss st here and there to add to the texture.

On the 25th row, k 2 tog at both ends, and repeat this on the 27th, 29th and 31st row, (8sts).
P alternate rows.
Continue in ss until the head is reached (about 10–12 rows) and cast off.
Make another piece in the same way. Press and sew up the side seams from the hem to ¾ in/2 cm from the top. Slip the undergown on to the figure and sew up the shoulders. Now fit the overgown on top of this and decorate with a large buckle as folls: use gold metallic yarn and cast on 10sts. Knit 3 rows in gt s and cast off, then gather one long edge into a circle. Glue this in place.

BEARD

In the white yarn, and size No14/2 mm needles, cast on 5sts and work in single rib for 6 rows. Inc one st at each end of the next 4 rows, (13sts).
Work 2 more rows in rib, then cast off in rib. Sew this round the lower face from ear to ear.

HAIR AND FACE

Cast on 20sts and work in single rib for 8 rows. Cast off in rib and sew one long edge around the head, leaving a bald patch on top. Embroider a pink nose, 2 blue eyes and thick white eyebrows.

HAT

Use No13/2¼ mm needles and cast on 28sts. Work 4 rows in ss.
5th row; (k 2 tog, k 5) 4 times.
6th and alt rows;p.
7th row; (k 2 tog, k 4) 4 times.
9th row; (k 2 tog, k 3) 4 times.
11th row; (k 2 tog, k 2) 4 times.
13th row; (k 2 tog, k 1) 4 times, (8sts).
Work 5 more rows in ss then (k 2 tog) 4 times.
Draw the last sts on to a thread and sew up. Allow the brim to curl upwards at the front, and sew on to the head with a firm back st.

STAFF

1 pc, doubled over at either end, will make the staff. Wrap tightly with the glittery yarn and sew it on to the wizard's hand.

MAGIC FOREST

Fairy folk, trolls, witches and
mythical creatures live in toadstool homes
and beneath talking trees,
deep in the heart of the magic forest.

FOREST

The magic forest is a perfect setting for the enchanted folk. Use lovely glittery yarns to create a magical effect.

Talking trees

The talking trees are enchanted creatures who were changed into trees by a magic spell and are waiting to be freed from their tree-bodies. They stand about 12 in/30 cm tall and the general pattern can be adpated in any way you choose, by colour, yarn texture, size and shape.

You will need No8/4 mm needles; any yarns, but double-knitting (DK) or thicker, is best - greens, browns and greys; cardboard tubes, about 9 in/23 cm tall with a diameter of 1¼ in/3 cm, a circular piece of thick card for the stand, about 3 in/8 cm diameter, either dark brown or dark green.

You will also need pliable but strong wire; for each tree you will need 4 pieces, each one about 20 in/51 cm long and one piece about 30 in/76 cm long, and a small pair of pliers and glue. Strong linen tape would be useful, but not essential, and a small amount of padding for the feet.

TO MAKE THE FRAME

1. Stick the base of the tube to the circle of card and allow to set (see Fig 29).]
2. Make the wire branches as folls:
   (a) Bend each piece of wire in half and bend the cut ends down with pliers, about ¾ in/2 cm and twist the 2 halves together to strengthen.
   (b) Make 8 small holes about ½ in/1.5 cm down from the top edge of the tube, just big enough to allow the doubled wires to pass through and no more. Space these equally apart.
   (c) Push the 4 wire pieces through the holes from one side to the other, so that there are 8 branches sticking out all round. Using the pliers, these should now be bent upwards to a vertical position for the time being. Do not tear the card while you are doing this!
   (d) At this point, wrap the linen tape once or twice round the top, over the wires and holes to strengthen this part.

KNITTED TREE COVER

This is the pattern for the moss stitch tree; the cable tree will need more sts and a cable needle.

Cast on loosely. Make a piece of knitted fabric to cover the tube, the above size will need a piece 4 in/10 cm wide. If thick DK yarn is used, and size 4 mm needles, 20sts will be needed. Finer yarn and/or needles will require more sts. Work in any textured st, such as double moss st or cables, and make the nose as follows:

Next row; patt 9sts, then inc 5sts into one st by making a k 1, p 1, k 1, p 1, k 1 all into the same st.

Knit 4 or 5 rows on these 5sts only, then dec back to one again. Continue along the row to the end.

Continue working to the top of the tube and then divide for the branches. Divide for 8 branches (for

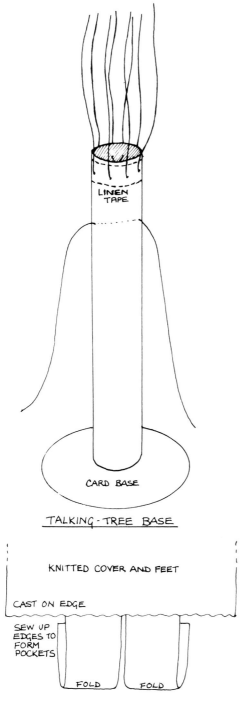

TALKING-TREE BASE

Fig 29: making the base for the talking trees

more than 20sts, adjust accordingly). Keep the 20sts on a stitch-holder or pin, and work 8 sets of sts individually, 4 sets of 3, and 4 sets of 2 *but* increase one st at the start of each set of 2 to make 3sts. These knitted branches should be as long as the wire branches and will enclose them when the tube is attached to the trunk. Use any st for the branches, garter or stocking. When casting off the 3sts, leave a long enough end of yarn to sew along each branch. When all 8 branches have been knitted, make the feet as follows.

Feet

Turn to the bottom of the knitted tree-cover and with the RS facing count 4sts in from the edge and pick up the next 5sts (i.e. from the cast-on edge) and knit 26 rows in gt s. Cast off, and pick up the next 5sts in the centre and knit another strip of 26 rows. Fold the strips in half and sew the two sides up, place a little padding inside the pocket thus formed and sew the cast-off edge to the trunk base (see Fig 29).

Making up

Take the piece of long wire and fold it in half, bending the 2 cut ends and twisting together as before. Make holes in each side of the card tube, about 2 in/5 cm from the top and insert the wire through the knitted cover and the card tube at the same time before sewing up. Pin the cover on to the tube and sew up the back seam, then enclose each wire branch in its knitted cover, fastening off each one securely. Bind each wire arm (i.e. the 2 lower ones) tightly round with thick oddments of yarn until the upper arm is as thick as a pencil and the lower part slightly thinner.

Now knit 2 covers for these arms with the same yarn as before, casting on about 34sts and working about 6 rows in ss, using the rev side as the RS. To make the piece wider at one end, k half a row, turn and p back. This will give 2 extra rows at one end. Position the coverings over the arms and pin in place, then sew firmly, stitching into the trunk at the 'shoulder' end. Embroider the eyes and mouth as shown.

Glue the lower edge of the trunk covering and the feet to the card base. Make a large floppy pom-pon using coarse green yarn and glue this to the top of the trunk inside the branches, pulling the ends well down over the head.

Small trees and bushes

These are perhaps the simplest of all to make. Cover a toilet-roll tube with a simple oblong of knitting, using gt s, ss, rev ss, or a textured yarn. Sew the two edges together and glue the piece in place, then add a huge, thick pom-pon of green, green/brown, russet or blossom-pink yarn. If the tree falls over easily, cut a small circle of thick card and glue this on to the base. The card tubes can be cut in half to make bushes. The pom-pons are glued to the tops.

Toadstool house

This can be seen on page 79. The overall height of the toadstool house is 7½ in/19 cm and its diameter is just over 6 in/15 cm. A circle of card will be needed for stiffening the top part, measuring 6 in/15 cm diameter exactly, and double-knitting yarns are used for the coverings, door and window, etc. Padding will be needed for the domed top.

TOP OF TOADSTOOL

Using gold-coloured yarn and size No10/3¼ mm needles, cast on 106sts, and work 10 rows in ss.
Row 11; (k 2 tog, k 8) 10 times, k 2 tog, k 4.
Row 12; purl on alternate rows.
Row 13; (k 2 tog, k 3) 19 times, (76 sts).
Row 15; (k 2 tog, k 3) 15 times, k 1, (61 sts).
Row 17; (k 2 tog, k 3) 12 times, k 1, (49 sts).
Row 19; (k 2 tog, k 3) 9 times, k 2 tog, k 2, (39 sts).
Row 21; (k 2 tog, k 6) 4 times, k 2 tog, k 5, (34 sts).
Row 23; (k 2 tog, k 6) 4 times, k 2 tog, (29 sts).

Row 25; (k 2 tog, k 6) 3 times, k 3, (25 sts).
Row 27; (k 2 tog, k 6) 3 times, k 1, (22 sts).
Row 29; (k 2 tog, k 2) 5 times, k 2 tog, (16 sts).
Row 31; (k 2 tog) 8 times, (8 sts). Draw these sts up to form the top, and stitch the two side edges together.

GILLS

Using brown yarn and size No10/3¼ mm needles, cast on 100 sts and work 10 rows, or 1¼ in/3.5 cm. Cast off and sew up the side seams.

STALK

Using stone coloured yarn, cast on 55sts and work in ss for about 5 in/13 cm. Cast off and sew up the side seams, slip this on to a tube of card. Assemble as shown in the diagram.

well over to the underside, holding it in place with pins. Lace across the back.

GILLS

In dark brown yarn, cast on 52sts using the same needles.
Work in k 2, p 2 rib for 8 rows, cast off in rib and sew up the two side seams.
Sew the cast on edge to the outer edge of the top.

STALKS

This is for a card tube which measures 2½ in long × 1½ in diameter/6.5 cm × 4 cm. Make a rectangle of fabric approximately 5½ in × 2½ in/14 cm × 6.5 cm. This one needs 34sts, double-knitting yarn, size No10/3¼ mm needles and 20 rows, but this should be checked against the tube.
See the diagram for assembling instructions.

Small toadstools

These can be seen on page 68 and 71.

TOP OF TOADSTOOLS

Using double-knitting yarn, and size No10/3¼ mm needles, cast on 50 sts and work 8 rows in ss. Then proceed as follows;
Row 9; (k 2 tog, k 3) 10 times, (40 sts).
Work 5 more rows in ss.
Row 15; (k 2 tog, k 2) 10 times, (30 sts).
Work 3 more rows in ss.
Row 19; (k 2 tog, k 1) 10 times, and purl the next row.
Row 21; (k 2 tog) 10 times.
Finish off by drawing a thread through the last sts and sewing up the two sides. Now cut a circle of stiff card 4 in/10 cm diameter, and stick a thick layer of padding to one side. Place the knitted top over this, and pull

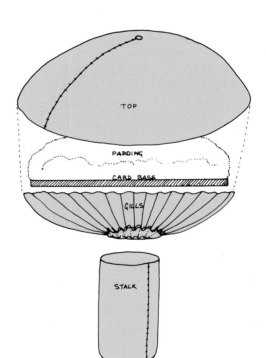

Fig 30: assembling the toadstool

FIGURES

Let your imagination run riot with a beautiful mixture of sparkling yarns. Instructions for making the wire frame bodies and knitted body coverings of the fairy folk are shown on pages 42 and 43. Picot pattern is used on some of the figures, see page 68. The diagrams for the wings shown on page 66 are general instructions and apply to all the fairies and elves.

*Oberon and Titania have discovered the Irish leprechaun
taking a rest under a bluebell.*

Fairy Wings

Take an 11 in/28 cm length of firm but bendable wire and twist the ends together as shown in *a*.

Shape into 2 wing-shapes – *b* – and twist each side once or twice – *c*.

Knit a rectangle of fine, glittery yarn just big enough to cover the wing area – *d*.

Attach the two outside edges of the knitting to the wire frame – *e*.

Gather the central area down towards the twisted parts – *f* – and continue to oversew the edges all the way round until the wire is completely covered.

Light, sparkling effects are obtained by combining fine crochet threads and fine gold threads made for machine sewing. Use size No10/3¼ mm needles to create a lacy, open effect.

The position of the wings on the fairy's shoulders are shown in *g*. Sew these very firmly.

Titania

Titania can be seen on page 65.

BODICE

A rectangle made in a mixture of a very fine Shetland wool, and any fine sparkling yarn.

Use size No15/1½ mm needles. Cast on 11sts, work 16 rows ss. Make 2 pieces and join at the shoulders and down the sides.

Stand-up collar

Size No15/1½ mm needles, any fine glitter yarn. Cast on 12sts. K 2 rows.

3rd row; inc into every other st all along the row.

K 2 more rows then change needles to size No10/3¼ mm, k 2 more rows and cast off. Sew the narrow edge around the neck, attaching the side edges to the shoulders.

SKIRT

Same yarn as bodice, No12/2¾ mm needles. Cast on 40sts.

Work 2 rows in ss then change to size No7/4½ mm

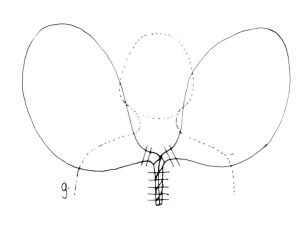

Fig 31: diagrams for wings

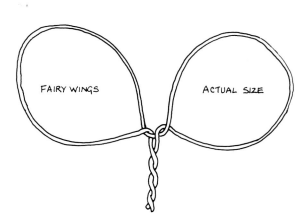

needles. Continue to the bottom for an ankle length skirt, introducing a band of gold yarn towards the last few rows.

UNDERSKIRT

This is a straight tube of fine white yarn from waist to ankles. Gather it around the waist and sew in place, then gather the top skirt and sew this over the top.

HAIR

This is a little cap of fine white moss st, (every row k 1, p 1 on an odd number of sts) shaped like a long rectangle. Size No14/2 mm needles. Cast on 25sts, and work 8–10 rows. Do not cast off but gather the last sts up to form the top of the hair, sew up the side edges and fit the cap well down on to the head. This is topped by a similar cap of glitter yarn, over which a crocheted chain band of gold thread has been sewn to resemble a delicate crown.

WINGS

Titania wears two pairs of wings, one of them smaller than the usual size, and these are covered loosely in a combination of crochet thread and fine glitter sewing thread.

WAND

Wrap a piece of fine wire with white yarn, folding the ends over sharply so that they are covered with yarn. Attach loops of glitter yarn to one end, then cut these to give a sparkling effect.Sequins may be added here and there.

Oberon

Oberon can be seen on page 64. The leg covering is of fine white yarn combined with metallic thread.

TUNIC

Made of double metallic thread. On size No15/1½ mm needles cast on 20sts.
Work in ss straight from hips to armholes, then divide for the arms.
Work 11 rows on the first 5sts.
Work 11 rows on the centre 10sts (this is the front).
Work 10 rows on the next 5sts, then k across all sts, thread these on to a length of yarn and gather. Slip the tunic on to the figure and sew up the back with the neck thread.

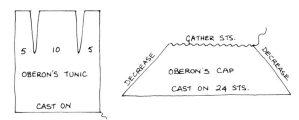

Fig 32: Oberon's tunic and cap

Collar

This is a crocheted braid of gold yarn fixed with a large sequin.

CAP

Cast on loosely, 24sts with silver yarn, and knit in ss to the shape shown in the diagram. Gather the last sts.

WINGS

Two pairs, one large and one small, made of glitter yarn and decorated with large silver sequins. Oberon's wings are about twice as big as the fairy's wings.

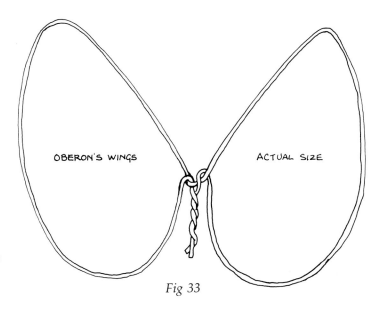

Fig 33

*The snowflake fairy's dress sparkles like the snow
and her tiny bonnet keeps her ears warm in the biting frost.*

Snowflake fairy

The leg covering is of fine white yarn. Picot pattern is used in her dress. It is worked as follows.

PICOT PATTERN

1st row; wool round needle to make one st, then *k 2 tog, and yarn forward* all along the row to the end, finishing with k 2 tog.

2nd row; purl.

These two rows form the pattern, making a row of holes which can be left open to make a lacy stitch, or folded over to make a pointed hem.

DRESS

White 2 ply baby wool combined with fine glitter yarn, with No15/1½ mm needles cast on 16sts. Work 4 rows in ss, then change to 2 rows of picot patt then work 14 more rows of ss.

Next row; k 2 tog all along the row, (8sts).

Next row; k 1, p 1.

Next row; change to aquamarine yarn and p 1, k 1. Continue in moss st for 6 rows then cast off. Make another piece in the same way. The front and back of the dress must now be completed *on the figure* as the

neck is not designed to fit over the head. Attach the back and front at one shoulder with 2sts, then fit these on to the figure and attach the shoulders at the other side. Leave the side seams free for the moment, these will be sewn up at the same time as the sleeve seam.

Sleeves

Using fine glitter yarn and aquamarine yarn, cast on 10sts and work in ss for 4 rows. Change to white yarn with glitter yarn.

Increase into every st (20sts) and work 5 more rows in ss.

Now work 2 rows of picot patt and cast off.

Sew up the sleeve seams, slip on to the arms and sew invisibly into the bodice, completing the side seam as you go.

HEAD-DRESS

Use fine white 2 ply and fine glitter yarn on No15/1½ mm needles.

Cast on 20sts and work 4 rows in ss then 2 rows picot patt and 8 more rows of ss. Gather the last sts on to a length of yarn and draw up. This is the back of the head-dress. Catch the two edges together with 2 or 3sts, and sew up half of the side edges – this gap fits around the back of the neck, with the cast-on edge framing the face. Sew in place and decorate the points of the picots with tiny pearl beads.

WINGS

She wears two small pairs of wings, one knitted with fine silver yarn and the other in white yarn but bound round the edges with fine silver yarn. Large needles give the openwork effect.

Daisy elf

Daisy and Daffodil elf are just two of the possibilities illustrated on the basic 'flower fairy' theme, wearing a simple tunic and hat, with leg coverings of the appropriate colour.

TUNIC

Random-dyed green 3 ply yarn, size No15/1½ mm needles. Make two pieces the same.

Cast on 14sts, work 16 rows of ss.

17th row; k 2 tog across all sts (7sts) then work 8 rows on these sts. Cast off. Sew up the sides from bottom to top as far as the decrease row, leaving the top part open for the arms. Stitch across the shoulders at x – 2 or 3 long sts should stretch across a gap of about ¼ in/1 cm which will be covered by the collar.

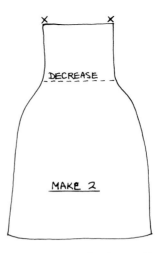

Fig 34: tunic for daisy elf

Collar

Green embroidery wool with fine glitter yarn.

Size No15/1½ mm needles, 20sts and 4 rows of ss.

Then work 2 rows of picot patt, and 6 more rows of ss. Fold up the picot hem and stitch in place, sew up the side edges and gather the cast on edge to fit around the neck. Sew in position.

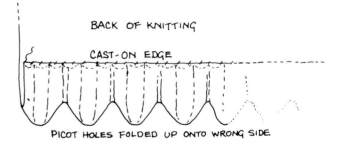

Fig 35: picot hem

DAISY HAT

Beginning with the yellow centre use 3 ply yarn and size No13/2¼ mm needles. Cast on 14sts and work 4 rows of ss.

Next row; k 2 tog all along the row (7sts) and gather these on to a length of yarn, sew up the side edges and stitch the cap to the top of the head.

Petal brim: use fine 2 ply white yarn combined with fine glitter yarn on size No13/2¼ mm needles. Cast on 28sts and work 6 rows in ss.

Work 2 rows in picot patt and then 8 more rows in ss. Fold up the picot hem and stitch in place and sew up the side seams. Gather the edge and sew this to the yellow crown of the hat, all the way round.

WINGS

Gold yarn.

Size No10/3¼ mm needles. Cast on 10sts and work 22 rows, (see page 66).

Daffodil elf

TUNIC

Yellow 3 ply yarn, size No10/3¼ mm needles.
Cast on 28sts, work 4 rows of ss, then 2 rows of picot patt.
Work 5 rows of single rib, beginning with a p st, then change needles to size No13/2¼ mm and rib 5 more rows.
Divide for the armholes: work 7 rows each on three divisions of 7, 14, and 7sts.

Gather the last sts on to a length of yarn and gather around the neck. Sew up the back seam.

HAT

Embroidery wool in orange, used double.
Size No13/2¼ mm needles. Cast on 20sts, work 4 rows of ss.
Next row; (k 2 tog, k 2) 5 times (15 sts).
P alternate rows.

The daffodil elf and the daisy elf take turns to ride on the ladybird,
who enjoys the fun as much as they do.

Forest elf lives among the trees and fungi of the woodlands.

Next row; (k 2 tog, k 1) 5 times.
Next row; (k 2 tog) to end of the row (5sts).
Draw these sts on to a length of yarn and sew up the side seam.

WINGS
These are the same as for the Daisy elf.

Forest elf

Mid-green leg covering.

TUNIC
Fine, pale green 3 ply yarn, size No13/2¼ mm needles.
Cast on 16sts, work 4 rows of ss, then change to picot patt for 12 rows, or as far as the armholes. Cast off.

Sleeves and top

These are made in one piece from one sleeve edge to the other. Cast on 14sts and work 4 rows in ss. Change to picot patt for 2 rows, * then work 6 more rows of ss. Divide for the neck opening: k 6, cast off 2sts, k 6. Work ss for 9 rows on each set of 6sts, then join across as follows: k 6, turn, and cast on 2sts, turn again, k 6. Purl across all 14sts. Now work in ss for 6 more rows, then 2 rows of picot patt, then 4 more rows of ss. Cast off and press lightly.

Fold up the picot hem on the sleeves, and sew up each sleeve seam *only* on the folded part of the hems, leaving the rest open for the lower tunic. Slip this part of the costume on to the figure. Sew up the back seam of the lower tunic, and slip this on to the figure, feet first. Sew the 2 pieces together from the right side. Stitch the neckline on to the figure, gathering it in a little at the same time if necessary.

HAT

Fine green 3 ply yarn, size No13/2¼ mm needles.
Cast on 18sts, work in ss for 4 rows.
Next row; (k 4, k 2 tog) 3 times.
Purl alternate rows.
Next row; (k 3, k 2 tog) 3 times.
Next row; (k 2 tog) to the end of the row, then gather these sts on to a length of yarn and sew the 2 side edges together. Sew the hat well down on to the head.

WINGS

One strand green embroidery wool combined with fine glitter yarn.
Size No10/3¼ mm needles.

Water elf

Two different tones of blue have been used for the leg covering in embroidery wool

TUNIC

The basic instructions for the tunic are the same as for the Forest elf, but here, the reverse of the fabric (the purl side) is the right side. However, the picot edge on the sleeves is still on the smooth side, so the following notes should be read before commencing.

Three strands of yarn were used together, 2 of embroidery wool (one blue and one white) and one strand of fine glitter yarn. Two different blues were interchanged at times to try to indicate a subtle movement of colour. Small pearls can either be threaded on to the yarn and knitted in, or sewn on afterwards.

Sleeves

White 2 ply baby yarn combined with fine glitter yarn. Work as for the Forest elf as far as *, then work 2 rows in ss.

Change to reverse ss by purling the next row and knitting the one after that until 8–9 rows after the picot patt are complete (i.e. instead of 6). Continue as for Forest elf but now read 'knit' instead of 'purl' and vice versa. Work rev ss for 6 rows on second sleeve, then change to ss by knitting row 7 and purling row 8.

Work 2 rows of picot patt, then 4 rows of ss. Cast off and press lightly.

Turn picot hems up on sleeve edges, remembering that you are using the reverse side of the fabric as the right side in this version. Finish off as for the Forest elf.

HAT

White 2 ply baby yarn combined with fine glitter yarn. This version is more pointed than the Forest elf's.
Cast on 18sts using No13/2¼ mm needles. Work ss for 8 rows, then continue as follows, purling on alternate rows;
Row 9; (k 4, k 2 tog) 3 times.
Row 11; (k 3, k 2 tog) 3 times.
Row 13; (k 2, k 2 tog) 3 times.
Row 15; (k 1, k 2 tog) 3 times (6sts).
Row 17; (k 2 tog) 3 times. Gather the last 3sts on to a thread and sew up.
Complete as for the Forest elf.

WINGS

As for the Forest elf, using blue yarn.

*Water elf likes to wander near flowing streams
and rivers, waterfalls and meadow ponds.*

*The gnome and his wife are industrious little creatures
who enjoy the warmth of a log fire when work is done.*

Gnome husband

Mid-green leg covering. Some padding inside the tunic will be needed to give the gnome a more rotund frame than the delicate fairies.

TUNIC

This is better explained in the diagram opposite as it is made in one complete piece, folded across the shoulders. A 3 ply yarn was used for this on size No14/2 mm needles.

Belt

This is made on 3sts in 3 ply yarn on size No15/1½ mm needles, in gt s. Make it long enough to go round the hips and sew the ends together at the back. The buckle is from a bra strap!

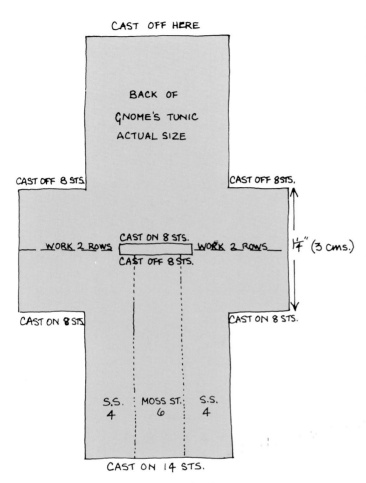

Fig 36: knitted tunic for the gnome

SEW SLEEVE
AND SIDE SEAMS
TOGETHER ON
BOTH SIDES

HAT

Cast on 20sts in 3 ply yarn on No15/1½mm needles, work in ss for 8 rows, then:

Row 9; k 2 tog, k 7, k 2 tog, k 7, k 2 tog.

Purl on alternate rows.

Row 11; k 2 tog, k 5, k 2 tog, k 5, k 2 tog, k 1.

Row 13; k 2 tog, k 4, k 2 tog, k 4, k 2 tog.

Row 15; k 2 tog, k 2, k 2 tog, k 2, k 2 tog, k 1. *

Row 17; (k 2 tog) 4 times (4sts).

Gather the sts on to a length of yarn, draw up and sew the sides together.

BAG

Use 3 ply brown yarn on No15/1½mm needles. Work in ss for 20 rows on 7sts. Now decrease one st at each end of the next 2 knit rows, then p one more row. Cast off the last 3sts, sew up the sides and stitch the flap down. Make a strap of crochet chain.

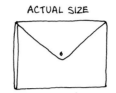

Fig 37: diagram of bag

BOOTS

Use brown 2 ply baby wool, cast on 14sts on No15/1½mm needles, work in ss for 20 rows. Thread the last sts on to the yarn and gather up to form the toe. Make another one to match.

Gnome wife

BODICE

The length of this should be measured against the figure for exact results. It consists of 2 small rectangles, one each for the front and back, joined at the shoulders leaving a space for the head to go through. Use 3 ply yarn and No15/1½mm needles. Cast on 10sts.

The short sleeves are 2 shallow rectangles of 10sts and 6 rows. These are joined to the bodice across the shoulders before the side and sleeve seams are sewn up. The white cuffs are of 2 ply wool on size No15/1½mm needles. Cast on 20sts. Work in ss for 10 rows, then cast off and join the side edges. Sew these to the lower edge of each sleeve.

SKIRT

This is a rectangle of grey 3 ply wool in ss. Use size No10/3¼mm needles and cast on 30sts. Measure it against the figure from the waist to the ankles, and introduce bands of rev ss and gt s at the lower edge. Sew up the sides and gather the top edge on to the bodice.

HAT

This is the same as for her husband, but uses grey wool. She also wears a scarf under her hat, but this need only be indicated by a long narrow strip of blue or any bright colour sewn around the head under the hat.

APRON

Use any colour 3 ply wool, cast on 10sts on size No13/2¼ mm needles. Work in ss for 14 rows, then cast off and sew the top edge to the centre portion of an 8 in/20 cm crochet chain.

LACE SHAWL

Use a fine white 2 ply on size No15/1½ mm needles, cast on 22sts and work in ss for 2 rows. On the 3rd row, inc in the first, then in every 3rd st to the end of the row (30sts). Inc one st at each end of the next k row, then p the next row. Change needles to size No10/3¼ mm and work 2 rows of ss.

Work 2 rows of picot patt, making the 2nd row knit instead of purl.

Cast off. Sew on to the figure as shown in the picture.

Brownie husband

Traditionally, these helpful little people are very poorly dressed; some even wear rags, though if new clothes are made for them and left as a gift, the brownies will never be seen again, though the clothes will disappear too! These brownies are reasonably well dressed compared to some others and do not like to be either thanked or taken for granted. Those which have become displeased by the treatment they receive have sometimes turned into hobgoblins and caused great mischief instead. The leg coverings are dark brown.

SHIRT

Made in one piece with the sleeves picked up from the side edges. Use 2 ply white baby yarn and size No14/2 mm needles. Cast on 14sts and work 12 rows of ss. Divide for the neck opening, leaving 7sts on each side. Work 9 rows on each side separately, then purl across both sets to make a complete row of 14sts again (rather like a large buttonhole). Continue in ss for 19 more rows, and cast off on the 20th row.

Sleeves

Pick up 12sts from the side edges and work ss for 8 rows, then cast off.

Sew up the sleeve and side seams, slip the shirt over the head and neatly stitch the lower edge of the shirt to the body all the way round.

WAISTCOAT

Use brown embroidery wool, size No15/1½ mm needles and work on 6sts and 12 rows in gt s. Cast off 3sts and k 10 more rows. Leave these sts on a spare needle and make another piece the same. Now knit across both sets of 3sts and continue down the back (see diagram below) on 6sts for 10 rows. Cast on 4sts at the beginning of the next 2 rows (14sts) and work 12 more rows in gt s. Cast off and join the side seams.

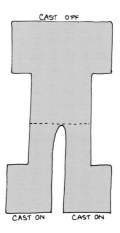

Fig 38: diagram of the brownie's waistcoat

*Once the housework is done, the brownies take
a few moments rest to admire the gleaming pans.*

HAT

This is the same as the gnome's hat except that the first 4 rows are worked in garter st.

SCARF

This version is crocheted on a foundation of 3 chains, but it can just as easily be knitted in gt s on 3 or 4sts for as long as you wish.

HAIR

Use 3 ply random-dyed brown wool, size No13/2¼ mm needles. Cast on 18sts and work 4 rows of gt s.
Next row; k 2 tog all along the row (9sts) then k one more row and gather the sts on to a length of yarn and sew up.

Brownie wife

The brownie wife does not wear shoes. She carries a duster in her hand, a sign of her willingness to do any task around the house. (See page 77).

SKIRT

Random-dyed yarn gives this rather shabby look to the skirt, but any fine 2 ply yarn will do just as well. Cast on 40sts, using No14/2 mm needles, and work in gt s for 2 in/5 cm. Gather the top edge after sewing up the side seam.

BODICE

This is knitted sideways, and has white sleeves attached to the sides.
Using brown yarn as for the skirt, cast on 18sts with No14/2 mm needles, and work in gt s for 4 rows.
Next row; k 7, cast off 4sts, k 7 (including the one left on the needle).
Knit 5 rows on the first set of 7sts, then join the yarn to the 2nd set and work 5 rows.
Next row; k 7, cast on 4sts, k 7, across all the sts, then k 5 more rows and cast off.

Sleeves

Knitted in white 2 ply baby wool on size No14/2 mm needles. Cast on 14sts, work 14 rows in ss.
Attach the cast-on edge of the sleeves to the bodice as shown in the diagram and sew up the sleeve and bodice seams. Slip over the head on to the body and gather under the gathered edge of the skirt. Sew the two pieces together.
Slip stitch the bodice neckline on to the figure.

APRON

With 2 ply white baby wool and size No14/2 mm needles, cast on 12sts and work 12 rows of ss, then 2 rows of picot patt, then 2 rows of gt s.
Cast off and make a crochet chain of 6 in/15 cm, which is then attached to the top edge of the apron.

DUSTER

This measures 2 in/5 cm square and is knitted in yellow embroidery wool on 20sts, size No15/1½ mm needles. Work 26 rows of ss or until square. Using a crochet hook, work 2 rows of double crochet around the edge. Then press flat.

HAIR

Use red-brown embroidery wool and size No15/1½ mm needles, cast on 20sts and work in single rib for ¾ in/2 cm then ss for 6 rows. Slip the last sts on to a thread and leave for the moment. Run a gathering thread along the line between the rib and the ss, draw up and fit this to the top of the head. Sew this piece in place. Insert a tiny piece of padding into the stocking st area. Draw up the thread and sew it up to form a bun.

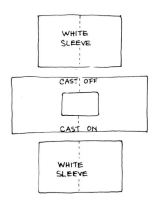

Fig 39: diagram of bodice and sleeves

Leprechaun

The lower legs are covered by white stockings and shoes knitted in one piece. Over the top edge of these he wears knee breeches. His quaint, old-fashioned dress is that of the well-known Irish fairy shoemaker, who is often seen wearing a three-cornered hat, though our version wears a simpler hat decorated with a sprig of shamrock, (see below, right).

SHIRT

Same as that of the brownie except that the sleeves have been made longer by 4 rows. Check on the basic figure to be exact about this.

KNEE BREECHES

Use a tweedy 3 ply Shetland wool in light brown, on size No13/2¼ mm needles. Cast on 12sts and work 22

The thin goblin waits for his friend to emerge from his toadstool house, while the leprechaun joins him for a chat.

rows in ss. Make 2 pieces the same. Sew up as shown in the diagram.

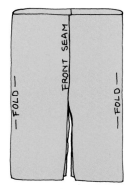

Fig 40: diagram of leprechaun's breeches

STOCKINGS AND SHOES

Using white 2 ply baby yarn and No15/1½ mm needles, cast on 14sts and work in ss for 16 rows, then change to dark brown yarn for the same thickness (double embroidery wool was used here) and work 10 more rows for the shoes. Gather the last sts on to the end of the foot and sew up. These should reach just above the knees. Sew them on to the legs, and draw the breeches over the top edge and catch them down. Run a gathering thread around the top of the shoes to draw them in to the ankles.

WAISTCOAT

This follows the same instructions as for the brownie, using green 3 ply yarn on No14/2 mm needles.

HAT

Use a 3 ply Shetland wool on size No14/2 mm needles, and cast on 18sts.
K 2 rows, p 1 row, k the next row.
Next row; (p 2 tog) 9 times (9sts), then k one more row. Cast off, then sew up and make a brim of crochet by working one double crochet into each cast off st all the way round the crown of the hat. With green wool, embroider (chain st) a band all the way round, and chain a sprig of green shamrock for his hat-band.

Thin goblin

Goblins are probably the least desirable of all the little people in this book, and traditionally they are portrayed as very ugly creatures. Our thin and fat goblins are not so much ugly as mischievous and rather cross-looking.
The leg coverings are purple.

TUNIC

This is made in a purple Shetland 3 ply on size No14/2 mm needles and 16sts. It is made to be sewn up the back. Follow the instructions as shown on the diagram, working in ss as far as the armholes (about 14 rows), then divide and work on the three sections separately for about 9 rows to the neck. Cast off and gather round the neckline.

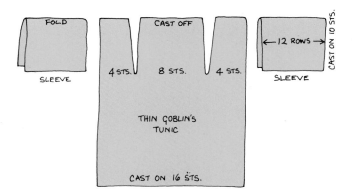

Fig 41: diagram of thin goblin's tunic

Sleeves

Cast on 10sts and work 12 rows; join the sides and stitch into the armhole of the tunic body. For the thin goblin, the tunic must be fitted on to the body before sewing up the back seam.

HAT

Use Shetland 3 ply wool on size No13/2¼ mm needles and cast on 20sts.
Work 8 rows in gt s, then follow the same instructions as for the gnome's hat as far as *, then ss for 6 rows. Then k 2 tog 4 times (4sts) and finish off. The front brim is turned up away from the face, and the back turned down.

BEARD

Use white 2 ply baby wool, size No14/2 mm needles and cast on 8sts, work 8 rows in single rib. Divide into 2 sections and work on each side separately on 4sts. Do not cast off, but gather the sts on to the cheeks underneath the hat.

The fat and thin goblins prepare to take a ride.

Fat goblin

Pad the body by wrapping it round the middle with narrow strips of padding. Bind these in position with thick yarn, (see page 81). The leg coverings are purple and the hat is the same as for the thin goblin. The beard is also the same, but it is gathered along the lower edge.

TUNIC

Follow the same instructions as for the thin goblin but double the number of sts to 32, using No13/2¼ mm needles. Knit one row and then change to size No11/3 mm needles and continue in ss for 14 rows.
Divide for the armholes 8sts–16sts–8sts.

Sleeves

The sleeves are also the same except that 12sts are worked instead of 10. Finish off in the same way as the thin goblin's version, but gather the edge of the tunic in with a thread and draw up gently towards the legs.

Belt

The belt is embroidered in chain st, using double yarn.

Rumpelstiltskin

This is the fairy character who, every night, spun heaps of straw into gold so that the young maiden could marry the king. She then found herself in the difficult position of having to guess his name. Here he is dressed in bright colours, each side of him different, as his character shows distinct traces of both charity and malevolence! He wears tights, a longish striped, multi-coloured tunic and a close-fitting hat with a pom-pon on top. His long hair and beard are the way he is usually represented.

TROUSERS

Using orange and yellow 3 ply yarns and size No14/2 mm needles, begin each leg as for the prince's breeches and boots on page 44, but working 32 rows in the same colour instead of 25 rows, and draw the last row up to form the toe.

TUNIC

The front and back are the same.
With No14/2 mm needles and orange, yellow and purple 3 ply yarns, cast on 12sts, beg at top and work 20 rows in ss (striped in 5 bands of 4 rows each). Change colour on a k row, then work 5 rows of single rib. Cast off in rib and make another piece in the same way.
Place the 2 pieces RS tog and make 2 or 3 sewing sts on each side of the shoulder seam, allowing enough room for the head to go through the opening.
With RS facing, pick up 14sts from the base of the 3rd stripe (i.e. from the shoulder) to the base of the 3rd stripe on the other side, along the side edge of the knitting. This is for the sleeve. Begin with a p row, and work 7 (striped) rows in ss.
8th row; (k 2 tog, k 1) 4 times, k 2 tog.
9th row; p.
Cast off, and work the other side in the same way.
Fold the garment RS's together and sew sleeve and side seams. Fit the tunic on to the figure and sl st the welt to the top of the legs, or leave free.

HAT

With No14/2 mm needles and 3 ply yarn, cast on 28sts, begin with a k row and work in rev ss for 2 rows, then change colour and work in ss (begin with a p row) for 5 rows.
Next row; (k 2 tog) 14 times.
Next row; p.
Next row; (k 2 tog) 7 times.
Thread these 7sts on to a length of yarn and gather up, using the same yarn to sew up the 2 edges for the back seam. Make a pom-pon of contrasting yarn and sew this to the top.

The troll and Rumpelstiltskin plot mischief under the pom-pon bush.

HAIR

With white yarn and size No14/2 mm needles cast on 18sts and work in single rib for 7 rows. Change to size No12/2¾ mm needles and work 2 more rows, then change to size No8/4 mm needles and work 4 more rows.

Next row; (k 2 tog, y fwd) 8 times, k 2 tog.

Next row; yrn, to make one st, then p.

Work 2 more rows in ss and cast off. Fold the cast off edge up, across the row of holes, to make a hem and sl st this in place. This is the lower edge of the hair. Sew this in place from one side of the face to the other leaving a bald patch on top.

BEARD AND FACE

With the same yarn and No14/2 mm needles, cast on 10sts and work in single rib for 1 in/5 cm. Now dec one st at each end of every alt row until only 2 sts rem. K 2 tog and darn the end into the beard.

Embroider the large pink nose and blue eyes, then sew the beard in place, placing a couple of sts into the hair at each side.

Sew the hat on to the head all the way round.

cast off and make another piece the same. These are the leg and breeches pieces. Sew them up as far as the top of the leg, insert the legs and then continue to sew the front and back seams.

TUNIC AND HEAD COVER

With mid-blue 3 ply yarn and the same needles, cast on 26sts and work in ss for 8 rows. Divide for the armholes as follows: work on the first 7sts, for 7 rows, then break off the yarn and join to the next section. Work on these 12sts for 7 rows. Break the yarn off again and work on the last 7sts for 7 rows, then p across all 26sts and then p one more row. Change to light-blue and p the next row.

Next row; (k 2, k 2 tog) 6 times, k 2.

Work 9 more rows in ss and draw the last row up on to a thread to form the top of the head.

Sew down the back from the top of the head to the waist, then run a gathering thread round the neck and draw up firmly. Sew the lower edge of the tunic to the breeches.

Sleeves

Cast on 12sts (mid-blue) and work 14 rows in ss. On the 15th row, p instead of k. Change to light-blue yarn and work 3 rows in ss beginning with a p row.

Troll

The troll is a Scandinavian-type creature, sadly misshapen, who lives in deep forests, mountains and under bridges. Remember the story of Billy-Goat Gruff? This one has blue skin to make him appear less human! The body framework will have to be adapted somewhat, but the diagram gives the rough size and shape of the figure without clothes. Pad and wrap it to form this bulky appearance, and make a blue skin cover instead of a pink one. The (bare) blue feet and breeches are knitted all in one piece, as are the body and head covering. Over this, he wears a dark hooded waistcoat. The hands and sleeves are also made all in one piece, see photo on page 83.

FEET AND BREECHES

With light-blue 3 or 4 ply yarn and No13/2¼mm needles, begin at the toe end, cast on 8sts and work 14 rows in ss; now change to mid-blue and work 2 rows. Now inc 1st at each end of the next 2 k rows, (12sts). Work straight until there are 14 mid-blue rows, then

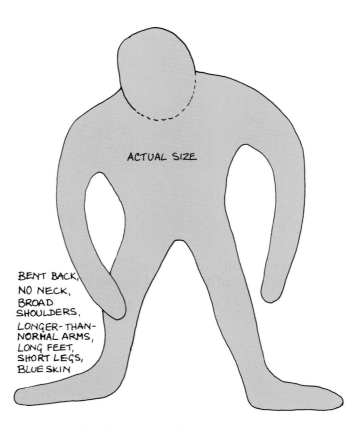

ACTUAL SIZE

BENT BACK, NO NECK, BROAD SHOULDERS, LONGER-THAN-NORMAL ARMS, LONG FEET, SHORT LEGS, BLUE SKIN

Fig 42: diagram of the body of the troll

Next row; (k 2 tog, k 3) twice, k 2 tog, (9sts).
Continue in ss for about 13 rows, or until the required length. Do not cast off, but draw the stitches up and sew the side seam, slip on to the arm and stitch to the tunic armhole. Make 2.

BEARD, HAIR AND FACE

Using No14/2 mm needles and white DK yarn, cast on 5sts and knit 5 rows in moss st then cast off. Sew the beard on to the bottom of the face, pulling the two sides up towards the ears. Embroider the hair with the same yarn, then embroider the features.

HOODED WAISTCOAT

Begin with the back piece, and with dark-blue yarn cast on 16sts and work 20 rows in ss.
Row 21; (k 2 tog, k 5) twice, k 2 tog
Row 22; p 13.
Row 23; k 2 tog, k 4, k 2 tog, k 3, k 2 tog.
Row 24; p 10.
Break off the yarn and leave these sts on a spare needle or stitch-holder. For the right front, cast on 10sts and work in ss except for the last 2sts on every p row which should be knitted. Continue straight for 20 rows.
Row 21; k 8, k 2 tog.
Row 22; p 7, k 2.
Row 23; k 7, k 2 tog.
Row 24; p 6, k 2.
Break off yarn and slip these sts on to a stitch-holder. For the left front, work as for the right front except that the 2 gt sts should be worked at the *beginning* of every p row instead of at the end. Reverse all shapings.
Now place all the stitches held on stitch-holders, in order, on to one needle and k across R front, back, and L front, beginning as follows:
Next row; cast off 4sts, k to end.
Next row; cast off 4sts, p to last 2sts, k 2.
Work on these 18sts for the hood for 12 more rows, keeping a border of gt s at each edge. Cast off, fold the hood in half across the top and sew together. Sew half-way up the side edges, leaving the open part for the arms.

STICK

Twist two pcs tightly together. Bend the doubled ends over at the top and bottom, and wrap tightly with brown yarn.

Dragon

In spite of great efforts on my part to make a really fearsome dragon, this dear little harmless creature emerged and now the other characters are by no means afraid of him, as they were meant to be! However, I feel that he fits into the scene rather well, and he is not difficult to make. As frame sizes may differ in the making, use a tape-measure to check measurements at all stages, and alter the pattern accordingly, see photo on page 87.
You will need No15/1½ mm, No13/2¼ mm and No12/2¾ mm needles; about 1oz/20gms bright orange 3 or 4 ply glittery yarn for the eyes; about 14pcs, sticky-tape, small pliers, strong bendable wire about 14 in/36 cm long, padding; 2 large cup-shaped sequins and 2 small glass beads for the eyes.

FRAME

(These numbers refer to those in Fig 43.)
1. Take 2 pipe cleaners, twist them together, fold in half at right angles as shown.
2. 2 more pcs twisted together 1½ in/4 cm from the left.
3. Place this twist at * in diagram No 4, and twist short ends round neck.
4. Strengthen back and neck with 2 more pcs laid alongside and twisted.
5. Use 2 pcs double, fold in half, place over body at base of neck for front legs and wrap round to hold in place. Twist legs to strengthen, and turn ends up.
6. Use 2 more pcs and do the same for the back legs, but make them shorter than the front.
7. Bow the legs wide apart and stand evenly.
8. Lengthen tail by twisting 2 pcs tog, and wrapping one end round the end of the body. Dragon frame should now measure about 9½ in/24 cm from the base of neck to tip of tail.
9. Lengthen head by folding 2 more pcs in half and overlap on to the neck by ¾ in/2 cm and bind in place with sticky-tape.
10. Bandage whole frame with long narrow strips of padding, making it thicker round the chest. Wrap in place with yarn.

KNITTED COVER

Main piece
Begin at the nose, and with size No13/2¼ mm needles cast on 12sts and work in gt s for 4 rows, then work 3 rows in ss.
Row 8; inc, k 5, inc, k 4, inc, (15sts).
Row 9; p.
Row 10; inc in every alt st to make 22sts.
Row 11; k.
Row 12; work in moss st for 10 rows.

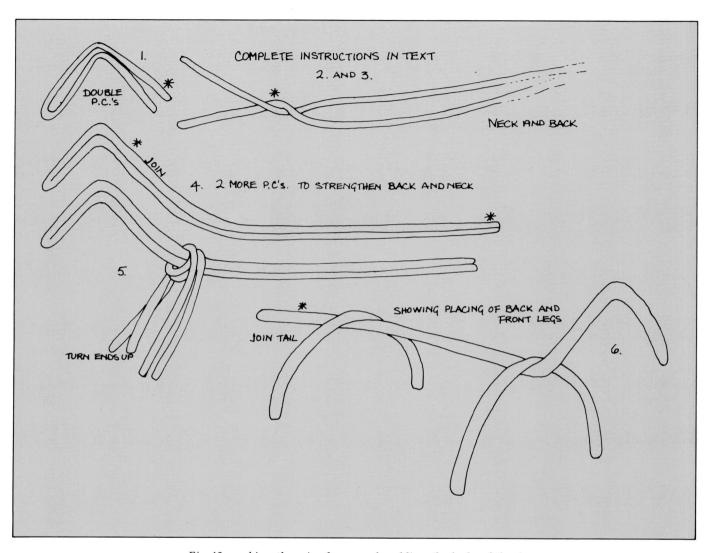

1. DOUBLE P.C.'s

COMPLETE INSTRUCTIONS IN TEXT
2. AND 3.

NECK AND BACK

4. 2 MORE P.C.'s. TO STRENGTHEN BACK AND NECK

JOIN

5.

TURN ENDS UP

JOIN TAIL

SHOWING PLACING OF BACK AND FRONT LEGS

6.

Fig 43: making the wire frame and padding the body of the dragon

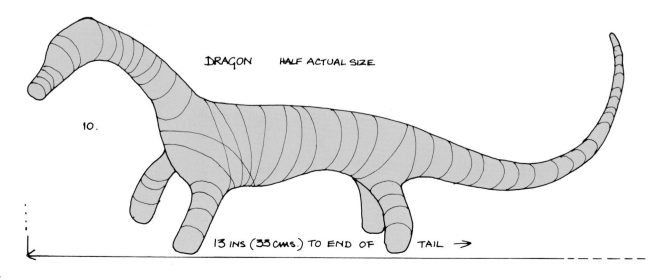

DRAGON   HALF ACTUAL SIZE

10.

13 INS (33 CMS.) TO END OF   TAIL →

The dragon tries to look fierce but his eyes sparkle like diamonds.

Row 22; work in double moss st for 6 rows.
Row 28; (k 2 tog, work 8sts) twice, k 2 tog, (19sts).
Keeping the patt correct, continue to the base of the neck (about 28 more rows).
Row 57; inc in first st (work 8 sts, inc) twice, (22sts). Work 2 more rows.
Rows 60 & 61; inc one st at each end of row.
Continue in double moss st for 12 more rows on these 26sts.
Row 74; dec one st at each end of this and every 4th row until 12sts rem.
Work 13 more rows on these 12sts, still in double moss st.
Cast on 3sts * at beg of next 2 rows and change to single moss st.
Work 4 rows without shaping on these 18sts.
Dec one st at each end of next and every foll 4th row until 10sts rem, and continue in moss st until this is nearly long enough to reach the tip of the tail, then dec one st at each end of alt rows until there are 2sts left. Cast off.
Gather the cast on sts on to a thread and draw up tightly. Sew the head up for about 1½ in/4 cm and sew up the same length at the tail end. Slip both ends on to the frame, leaving the yarn uncut so that sewing can continue later.

Legs and underside gusset
Begin at the neck end, and with size No12/2¾ mm needles cast on 2sts. Work in ss, inc one st at each end of every alt row until there are 12sts. Cast on 8sts at beg of next 2 rows, (28sts). Work 12 more rows, then cast off 8sts at beg of next 2 rows. Continue in ss for 24 rows, or until this piece is long enough to reach the back legs.
For the back legs, cast on 8sts at beg of next 2 rows.
Next row; k 13, k 2 tog, k 13.
P alt rows and dec one st in the centre of every k row until 21sts rem.
[Note: on every alt decrease row, there will be an uneven number of sts at each side of the decrease sts.]
Cast off 8sts at beg of the next 2 rows, then cast off the last 5sts.
Fold the 4 legs in half (downwards) RS together, and sew up the leg seams. Turn RS out and slip these on to the dragon framework, pinning the neck point and the 2 sides in position. Twist the leg seams slightly towards the back. Match up the edges of the upper and lower pieces and pin together along both sides. These must be sewn up while on the framework, from the RS, so care must be taken to make the sts as invisible as possible. Pin the 3 extra sts * underneath the base of the tail, and sew (see Fig 44).

WINGS
With size No15/1½ mm needles, cast on 4sts and work 4 rows in single rib. Now inc at the beg of every alt row until there are 14sts. Work 1 more row and then cast off in rib. Make 2.
Take a piece of strong but bendable wire 7 in/18 cm long and fold it in half, pinching the bend with pliers and gently twisting the rest together. Bend this piece into a right angle, and lay this alongside the right angle of the knitted piece. Using the same yarn, bind the

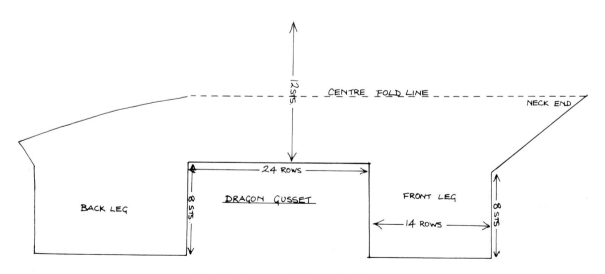

Fig 44: diagram of the underside gusset

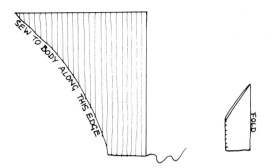

Fig 45: diagrams of the dragon's wings and ears

wire to the edge of the knitting, covering the wire completely with yarn. Sew these wings to each side of the body at the shoulders, (see Fig 45).

EARS

With size No15/1½ mm needles, cast on 8sts and work in ss for 4 rows. Dec one st at each end of every k row until only 2sts rem. Cast off. Make 2. Fold ears along centre line and sew up the 2 short edges, leaving the tops open. Point the ears towards the front, pin on to head and sew firmly.

EYES

Using glittery (or other contrasting) yarn, and size No15/1½ mm needles, cast on 8sts and work in gt s for enough rows to make a ¾ in/2 cm square. Cast off. Make 2. Place a small piece of padding in the centre and gather the edges round the padding and press flat. Sew these pads to each side of the head and finish off with a large cup-shaped sequin held on with a small glass bead.

Unicorn

This beautiful and mythical creature is more the size of a pony than a horse, and differs from the latter in several ways, (see Fig 46). Apart from its spiral horn, it has a goat's beard, cloven hooves like a deer, and a lion's tail. This knitted version has hooves of gold as they are too small to show the cloven effect, see photo on page 91.

You will need No14/2 mm and No12/2¾ mm needles and a small crochet hook to hook the mane into the neck; 4 ply cream or white (less than 1oz/20 gms) and tiny amounts of pink and blue yarns, and metallic gold for the hooves. Some fine glitter yarn may be knitted in

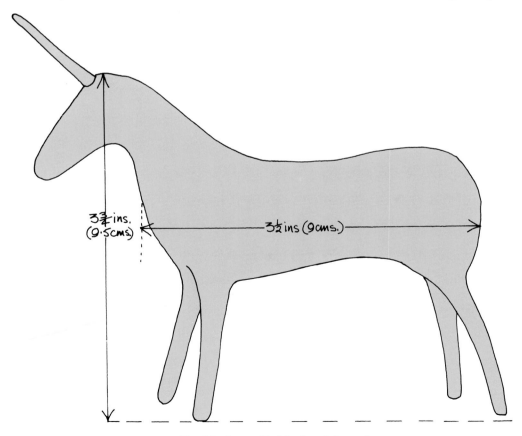

Fig 46: the padded body of the unicorn

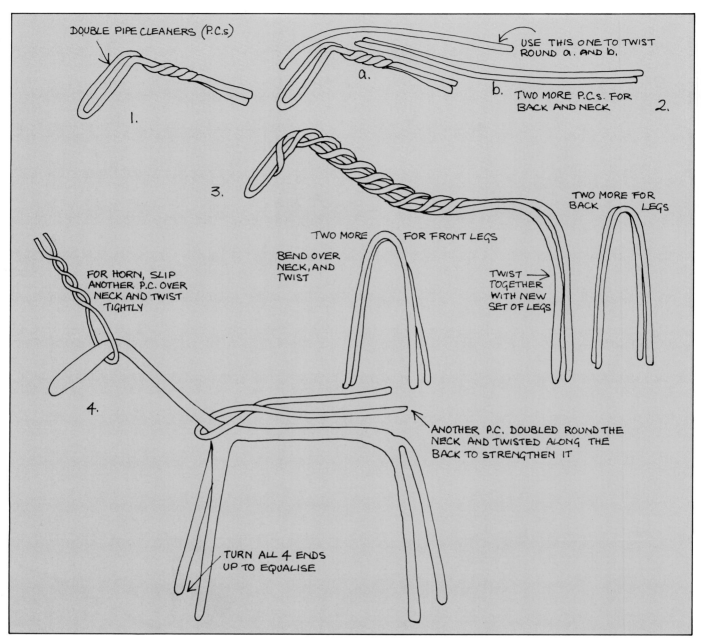

Fig 47: making the wire frame for the unicorn

for the horn, and into the mane. For the frame you will need about 11 pcs, padding and thick white yarn for wrapping, (see Fig 47).

KNITTED BODY COVERING

Front legs
*Using No14/2 mm needles and gold yarn for the hooves, cast on 8sts and k 4 rows in gt s then change to white yarn and k 1 row.
Change to size No12/2¾ mm needles and work in ss* for 12 more rows.

Now cast on 2sts at beg of next 2 rows. Cast off. Make 2. Sew up the seams and slip the leg coverings in place, turning the seam towards the back.

Back legs
Work from * to * as for the front legs then work for 16 more rows, and finish in the same way as for the front legs. Make 2.

Body covering
Use size No12/2¾ mm needles and white yarn, and begin at the nose end.

90

The unicorn is a mythical creature
who has dainty golden hooves and sparkling eyes

Cast on 12sts and work in ss for 2 rows, then inc at each end of every k row until there are 18sts, ending with a p row. Now make a hole for the horn (you may have to adjust the placing of this).

Next row; inc in first st, k 7, cast off 2, k 7, inc in last st.
Next row; p 9, turn and cast on 2sts, turn and p 9.
Continue increasing in first and last sts until there are 24sts then p the next row.

Shape neck

Inc in first st, k 13, leave 10sts on LH needle, turn and p 4. Turn and k 6, turn and p 8, turn and k 10, turn and p 12, turn and k 14, turn and p 16, turn and k to last st, inc one st. Now p across all sts.

Continue to inc as before until there are 30sts, then work straight for 9 more rows.
Next row; k 2 tog, (k 12, k 2 tog) twice.
Continue without shaping for 12 rows.
Next row; inc in first st, (k 12, inc) twice.
Next row; k 18, turn, leaving 12sts on LH needle, p 6, turn and k 9, turn and p 12, turn and k 15, turn and p 18, turn and k to the end of the row. Now p one more row.
Next row; k 2 tog across all sts (15sts).
Next row; p 15.
Gather these 15sts on to the attached yarn and draw up.

MAKING UP

1. First attach the leg coverings, keeping the seams of the front ones towards the back, and those on the back ones towards the insides. Stitch the top edges to the body-padding, pulling them high on to the body with the stitches.

2. Gather the nose-end (i.e. the cast on edge) of the body-covering and secure with one or two stitches, then sew neatly along the under-head/neck seam as far as the increases. This is the lower point of the chest, at the top of the two front legs.

3. Slip this part on to the frame, slipping the horn through the hole in the head part. Fit it snugly on to the head and chest, and pull the back curve over the back end of the body. Bring the two gathered edges together under the body at the top of the two back legs, and pin in position. Draw the edges together under the rest of the body, round the front legs, and pin. Sew neatly in position.

4. The horn should now be trimmed to about 1¼ in/ 3 cm long and a cover knitted using a fine 3 ply yarn or a fine metallic yarn. Use size No14/2 mm needles and cast on about 8–10sts and knit the length of the horn, tapering towards the end. Sew, from the point downwards, inserting the horn when only about half has been sewn up so that the lower half can be sewn and shaped 'in situ'. Sew firmly in position.

5. The ears are made from the same yarn as the body, using fine needles on about 5sts. Work 4 rows of ss then k 2 tog, k 1, k 2 tog, and on the next row, p 3, then k 2 tog, k 1, and cast off.

6. The tail should be more like a lion's tail than a horse's and so can be a knitted strip with a tassel sewn on to the end. Sew it well up on to the top of the rump.

7. The mane is made up from short lengths of yarn hooked through the sts along the top of the neck. Make this as thick as possible, and if it will not lie down as a mane should, it is probably better to allow it to stand up.

8. The beard, like a goat's, is just a cluster of threads hooked underneath the chin.

9. Embroider the eyes and pink nostrils as shown.

Ladybird

Ladybirds and other beetles, grasshoppers and butterflies are all used by the fairies in the same way that humans use horses. A ladybird can easily carry two or three fairies.

Double knitting yarn is used for the ladybird; small amounts of red and black are required, some firm wire for the legs and two black beads or buttons for the eyes. Small pieces of card are needed for the stiffening and base. Padding is also needed.

Use size No11/3 mm needles, cast on 30 sts in red yarn. Work 28 rows in ss.
Change to black and work 2 more rows, then (k 2 tog, k 3) 6 times.
Purl the next row, then (k 2 tog, k 2) 6 times (18sts).
Continue in ss for 9 more rows, gather the last sts on to a thread and draw up tightly. Stitch the gathers together and pull this section over the head end of the card base. Gather the cast-on edge, stitch together, and pull this over the tail end. Pad between the card and the knitting, and lace across the back.
The legs are made from three pieces of wire each measuring about 7⁄8 in/8 mm long. These pieces are wrapped with black yarn and bent over at the ends as shown in the diagram. They are stitched on to the underside slightly towards the head end, and the smaller base card is then stuck over the top.

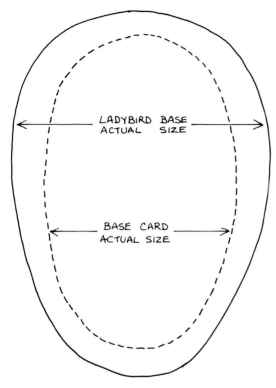

Fig 48: the base for the ladybird body

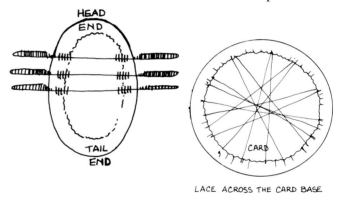

Fig 49: completing the ladybird's body and legs

This is by no means the end of the story.
The enchanted characters illustrated here are only a few of those who may be encountered by mortals, and their individual appearance will vary greatly depending on their place of origin.
Every fairy tale will give a different description. The solution is to take the essential ingredients of the characters and then use your imagination as I have done in this book. Use the basic shapes to create your own fantasy story. It will give great pleasure to your friends and help to rekindle a world of magic and fun.

Helping hand

If you are a complete beginner at knitting, or your skills are a little rusty, the following information will be helpful.

Place the needle holding the stitches in the left hand and hold the working needle and the yarn in the right hand. Control the yarn by winding it round the fingers of the right hand, (see Fig 50).

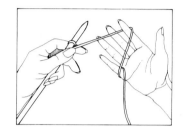

Fig 50 controlling the yarn tension

CASTING ON

Begin with a slip loop about 15 cm (6 in) from the end of the yarn and tighten it on to the left-hand needle (see Fig 51). Insert the right-hand needle into the front of the loop, left to right, wind the yarn round the right-hand needle point and draw it through to the front (see Figs 52 and 53). Transfer the loop from the right-hand needle to the left-hand needle. Continue in this way, but insert the needle *between* the stitches on the left-hand needle, (see Fig 54), until you have the correct number of stitches.

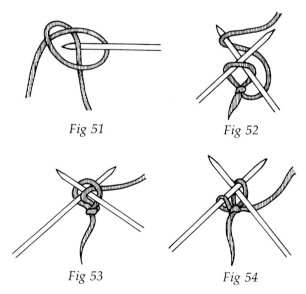

Fig 51 *Fig 52*

Fig 53 *Fig 54*

TO KNIT STITCHES

Hold the yarn at the back of the work. Insert the right-hand needle into the first stitch on the left-hand needle from front to back, left to right (see Fig 55). This is known as 'knitwise'. Pass the yarn round the right-hand needle point, (see Fig 56) and draw the loop through to the front of the work, (see Fig 57). Slip the stitch off the left-hand needle (see Fig 58). Continue in this way along the row until you have transferred all the stitches to the right-hand needle. Turn the work and hold it in the left hand in preparation for the next row.

Knit stitch

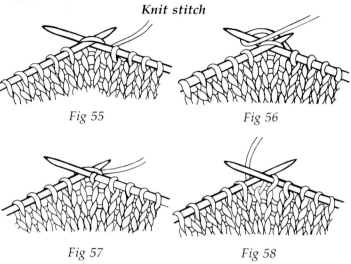

Fig 55 *Fig 56*

Fig 57 *Fig 58*

TO PURL STITCHES

With the yarn at the front of the work, insert the right-hand needle into the front of the first stitch on the left-hand needle from right to left (see Fig 59). This is known as 'purlwise'. Pass the yarn round the right-hand needle point (see Fig 60). Draw the loop through (see Fig 61), then slip the stitch off the left-hand needle (see Fig 62). Continue in this way along the row.

Purl stitch

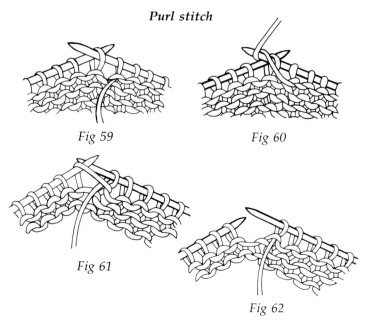

Fig 59 *Fig 60*

Fig 61

Fig 62

Index

CHEESECAKES
SWEET & SAVORY

CHEESECAKES
SWEET & SAVORY

Barbara Maher

CONTENTS

ANOTHER BEST-SELLING VOLUME FROM HPBooks®
Publisher: Rick Bailey; Editorial Director: Elaine R. Woodard
Editor: Jeanette P. Egan; Art Director: Don Burton
Book Assembly: Leslie Sinclair
Typography: Cindy Coatsworth, Michelle Carter
Director of Manufacturing: Anthony B. Narducci
Recipe testing by International Cookbook Services: Barbara Bloch,
President; Rita Barrett, Director of Testing; Nancy Strada, Tester

Published by HPBooks, Inc.
P.O. Box 5367, Tucson, AZ 85703   602/888-2150
ISBN 0-89586-349-9
Library of Congress Catalog Card Number 85-68379
© 1985 HPBooks, Inc. Printed in the U.S.A.
1st Printing

Originally published as Tempting Cheesecakes
© 1985 Hennerwood Publications Limited

Cover Photo: Strawberry & Sour-Cream Cheesecake, page 31

Introduction

Although cheesecakes have been eaten in the Middle East for centuries, it is only in recent times that they have had widespread popularity. The early cheesecakes were always baked. They usually consisted of a pastry base filled with a soft cheese enriched with eggs, sugar or honey and enhanced with spices or aromatic flavorings. This tradition has been maintained and encouraged by European cooks. The first Europeans to eat cheesecakes were probably the Romans. Later European cooks introduced new ingredients, such as fresh and candied fruit, nuts and liquors.

Unbaked cheesecakes are a comparatively recent introduction. They are quite different from baked cheesecakes. They usually have a crunchy cookie-crumb base and a creamy filling containing gelatin.

Here is a worldwide selection of cheesecake recipes from Austria, Hungary, France, Russia, Germany, Switzerland and the United States. Some recipes will be familiar, such as classic *Lindy's Style Cheesecake*. Others will be less well known and delicious surprises.

When done, a baked cheesecake should have risen and be golden brown. Test by inserting a skewer or wooden pick slightly off center. The skewer or pick should come out clean and dry. If any mixture adheres, bake the cheesecake a few minutes longer. The center is always the slowest part to cook. However, the center of the cheesecake will continue to cook as it cools; for this reason do not insert skewer or pick in center of cheesecake.

Baked cheesecakes have a tendency to crack as they bake. These cracks may almost disappear as the cheesecake deflates and cools. This does not affect the texture or flavor. It is simply a characteristic of some baked cheesecakes.

TYPES OF CHEESE

Most of the cheesecakes in this book are made with cream cheese which has a butterfat content of about 33 percent. Cream cheese gives cheesecakes a good flavor and texture; it does not mask the flavor of the other ingredients. Use equal amounts of cream cheese and cottage cheese to reduce the amount of fat, if desired.

Neufchâtel cheese is similar to cream cheese, but is lower in fat content. It can be substituted for cream cheese in most recipes.

Cottage cheese should be thoroughly drained before using. Cottage cheese has a fat content of 4 percent or less. Ricotta cheese, the Italian equivalent of cottage cheese, is also low in fat. Cottage cheese and ricotta cheese both spoil quickly. They are best when very fresh. Like cottage cheese, ricotta cheese should also be well drained before using. For a smoother texture, process cottage cheese or ricotta cheese in a blender or food processor with a steel blade before using.

EGG WHITES

Beating egg whites—Always beat whites in a spotlessly clean bowl. Even a hint of fat will prevent the egg whites from beating properly. For best results use a whisk or an electric beater. Start by beating slowly. As the whites froth up, increase the speed. The object is to incorporate as much air as possible.

Beaten egg whites should stand in stiff but not dry peaks. A rubber spatula pulled through the beaten egg whites will leave a gap. Overbeaten egg whites are granular and slightly lumpy in appearance. They quickly start to separate and become watery. At this stage they are unusable. Discard and start again with fresh egg whites.

To beat in sugar, beat egg whites until soft peaks form. Gradually beat in sugar; beat until stiff and glossy.

Folding in beaten egg whites—Fold in beaten egg whites as soon after beating as possible. Use a large metal spoon or a spatula for folding. Spoon the beaten egg whites onto the cake mixture.

To fold, bring the spatula or spoon down through the eggs whites and cake mixture, across the bottom and back up the opposite side against bowl. Repeat until no egg-white streaks remain. Do not overfold or the air beaten into the egg whites will be lost.

If the cake mixture is very stiff, stir in one-fourth to one-third of the beaten egg whites. Then fold in the remaining beaten egg whites. To fold beaten egg whites into a gelatin mixture, refrigerate the mixture until it mounds when dropped from a spoon. Then carefully fold in egg whites.

Basic Recipes

Nut-Crumb Crusts

Crust for an 8-inch springform pan:
3/4 cup graham-cracker crumbs
1/4 cup finely ground almonds or other nuts
2 tablespoons sugar
1/4 teaspoon ground cinnamon, if desired
2 tablespoons butter or margarine, melted

Crust for a 9-inch springform pan:
3/4 cup graham-cracker crumbs
1/2 cup finely ground almonds or other nuts
5 tablespoons sugar
1/2 teaspoon ground cinnamon, if desired
1/4 cup butter or margarine, melted

Crust for a 10- or 11-inch springform pan:
1 cup graham-cracker crumbs
1/2 cup finely ground almonds or other nuts
6 tablespoons sugar
1/2 teaspoon ground cinnamon, if desired
6 tablespoons butter or margarine, melted

---

1. Grease bottom and side of pan.
2. In a small bowl, combine crumbs, nuts, sugar and cinnamon, if desired. Stir with a fork until blended. Stir in butter or margarine until combined.
3. Press crumb mixture evenly onto bottom of lined pan, smoothing with back of a spoon. Refrigerate crust while preparing filling.

Vanilla Sugar

A jar of vanilla-scented sugar is always useful in the kitchen. It can be used to give a subtle and authentic vanilla flavor that is superior to synthetic vanilla extract. To make vanilla sugar, fill a jar with sugar. Place a vanilla bean in center of sugar. Seal airtight. Store in a cool place. One vanilla bean will flavor 2 pounds of sugar. Vanilla sugar will keep about a year. As the sugar is used, simply fill jar with more sugar. Use vanilla sugar in place of sugar and vanilla extract.

Crumb Crusts

Crumb Crust for an 8-inch springform pan:
1 cup graham-cracker crumbs
1/4 cup granulated sugar or firmly packed light-brown sugar
1/2 teaspoon ground cinnamon
1/4 cup butter or margarine, melted

Crumb Crust for a 9-inch springform pan:
1-1/4 cups graham-cracker crumbs
1/3 cup granulated sugar or firmly packed light-brown sugar
1/2 teaspoon ground cinnamon
6 tablespoons butter or margarine, melted

Crumb Crust for a 10- or 11-inch springform pan:
1-1/2 cups graham-cracker crumbs
1/2 cup granulated sugar or firmly packed light-brown sugar
1 teaspoon ground cinnamon
1/2 cup butter or margarine, melted

---

1. Grease bottom and side of pan.
2. In a small bowl, combine crumbs, sugar and cinnamon. Stir with a fork until blended. Stir in butter or margarine until combined.
3. Press crumb mixture evenly onto bottom of lined pan, smoothing with back of a spoon. Refrigerate crust while preparing filling.

Variations
Chocolate- or Vanilla-Crumb Crust: Substitute crushed chocolate or vanilla wafers for graham-cracker crumbs. Reduce sugar as follows. For an 8-inch pan, reduce sugar by 2 tablespoons. For a 9-inch pan, reduce sugar by 3 tablespoons. For a 10- or 11-inch pan, reduce sugar by 1/4 cup. Omit cinnamon, if desired. Use same amount of butter or margarine.

For a firmer crust, bake in a preheated 350F (175C) oven 10 minutes. Cool completely before filling.

Shortcrust Pastry

1-1/4 cups all-purpose flour
1/2 teaspoon salt
1 tablespoon sugar, if desired
1/2 cup butter or margarine or 1/4 cup butter or
    margarine and 1/4 cup vegetable shortening
1 egg yolk
1 to 2 tablespoons iced water

1. In a medium bowl, stir flour, salt and sugar, if desired, until blended. With a pastry blender or 2 knives, cut in butter or margarine or butter or margarine and shortening until mixture resembles coarse crumbs.
2. In a small bowl, combine egg yolk and 1 tablespoon iced water. Sprinkle over flour mixture; toss with a fork until mixture binds together. Stir in remaining water, if necessary. Knead pastry in bowl several strokes or until smooth.
3. Shape pastry into a flattened ball; wrap in plastic wrap. Refrigerate 30 minutes.
4. Preheat oven to 425F (220C). Lightly grease an 8- or 9-inch springform pan. On a lightly floured surface, roll or pat out pastry. Use pastry to line bottom and side of pan, pressing pastry about 1 inch up side of pan. **To bake blind,** prick with a fork. Line with foil; fill with pie weights or dried beans.
5. Bake in preheated oven 10 minutes. Remove foil and pie weights. Reduce oven temperature to 375F (190C). Bake 5 to 6 minutes more or until pastry is golden brown. Cool in pan on a wire rack before filling. Makes an 8- or 9-inch pastry shell.

Sweet Shortcrust Pastry

1-1/2 cups all-purpose flour
3 tablespoons sugar
1/2 teaspoon grated lemon peel
1/4 teaspoon salt
1/2 cup butter or margarine
1 egg yolk
2 to 3 tablespoons iced water

1. In a medium bowl, combine flour, sugar, lemon peel and salt. With a pastry blender or 2 knives, cut in butter or margarine until mixture resembles coarse crumbs. In a small bowl, combine egg yolk and 2 tablespoons iced water. Sprinkle over flour mixture. Stir with a fork to make a soft, but not sticky dough. Stir in remaining water, if necessary.
2. Shape pastry into a flattened ball; wrap in plastic wrap. Refrigerate 30 minutes.
3. Preheat oven to 400F (205C). **To line a springform pan with pastry,** grease a 9- or 10-inch springform pan. On a lightly floured surface, roll or pat out pastry to fit pan. Line bottom and side of pan, pressing pastry 1 inch up side of greased pan. **To bake blind,** prick pastry with a fork. Line with foil; fill foil with pie weights or dried beans.
4. Bake in preheated oven 10 minutes. Remove foil and pie weights. Reduce oven temperature to 375F (190C). Bake 5 to 7 minutes more or until pastry is golden brown. Cool in pan on a wire rack before filling.
5. To make tart shells, divide pastry into 12 equal pieces. On a lightly floured surface, roll or pat out each piece of pastry to fit tart pans. Use pastry to line 12 (3-1/4-inch) tart pans, pressing pastry into fluted sides of pans. Prick pastry all over with a fork. Bake in preheated oven 12 to 15 minutes or until golden. Cool in pans on a wire rack before filling.
6. Makes 1 (9- or 10-inch) pastry shell or 12 tart shells.

Baking Blind

Pastry for cheesecakes is usually baked before filling to prevent a soggy crust. Grease pan; line bottom and side with pastry. Prick all over with a fork. Press a sheet of foil lightly over pastry; fill foil with dried beans or pastry weights. These can be used again and again for this purpose. The weights prevent pastry from puffing during cooking.

Bake in a preheated 400F (205C) oven 10 minutes. Reduce oven temperature to 375F (190C). Remove foil and weights. Bake 5 to 7 minutes more. Cool in pan on a wire rack before filling.

Yeast Dough

1 (1/4-oz.) pkg. active dry yeast (1 tablespoon)
1/4 cup plus 1 teaspoon sugar
2/3 cup warm milk 110F (45C)
2 eggs, beaten
6 tablespoons butter or margarine, melted, cooled
1 tablespoon grated lemon peel
1/2 teaspoon salt
About 2-3/4 cups all-purpose flour

1. In a large bowl, dissolve yeast and 1 teaspoon sugar in warm milk. Let stand 5 to 10 minutes or until foamy.
2. Beat in eggs, butter or margarine, remaining 1/4 cup sugar, lemon peel and salt until blended. With a wooden spoon, stir in 2-1/4 cups flour to make a soft dough that comes away from side of bowl.
3. On a lightly floured surface, knead in enough remaining flour to make a stiff dough. Knead 8 to 10 minutes or until dough is smooth and elastic.
4. Clean and grease bowl. Place dough in greased bowl; turn to coat sides. Cover with a slightly damp towel. Let rise in a warm place, free from drafts, 1 hour or until doubled in bulk.
5. Punch down dough; use as directed in recipe. Makes enough dough to line bottom and side of a 10- or 11-inch springform pan.

Cheese & Spinach Filo Rolls, page 71

Sponge Layer

5 eggs
2/3 cup sugar
1 tablespoon grated lemon peel
1 cup cake flour

1. Preheat oven to 350F (175C). Grease a 9-, 10- or 11-inch springform pan. Line bottom of pan with parchment paper or waxed paper; grease paper. Dust bottom and side of pan with flour; tap out excess flour.
2. In a medium bowl, beat eggs and sugar 10 minutes or until thick and lemon-colored and mixture falls in a thick ribbon when beaters are lifted. Beat in lemon peel.
3. Gradually sift flour over egg mixture, folding in while sifting. Pour mixture into prepared pan; smooth top.

4. Bake in preheated oven 25 to 30 minutes or until center springs back when lightly pressed. Cool in pan on a wire rack 10 minutes. Run tip of a knife around inside edge of pan to release cake. Remove from pan; invert cake onto a rack. Peel off lining paper. Cool completely on wire rack. Use as directed in recipe.
5. To make ahead, wrap cooled cake in plastic wrap or foil; store in an airtight container up to 2 days. Or, freeze up to 2 months. Thaw at room temperature 1 hour before using. Makes 1 (9-, 10- or 11-inch) cake layer.

Variation
Chocolate Sponge Layer: Reduce flour to 3/4 cup; add 1/4 cup unsweetened cocoa powder. Sift flour and cocoa over egg mixture. Continue as directed above.

Raspberry Bagatelle, page 54

Genoise Sponge

5 eggs, separated
3/4 cup sugar
1 teaspoon grated lemon peel
1 cup sifted cake flour
1/2 cup butter or margarine, melted

---

1. Preheat oven to 350F (175C). Grease a 10- or 11-inch springform pan. Line bottom with parchment paper; grease paper. Dust bottom and side of pan with flour; tap out excess flour.
2. Place egg yolks and sugar in a large bowl set over a pan of simmering water. Let stand about 5 minutes or until warm to the touch. Beat egg yolks and sugar about 10 minutes or until thick and lemon-colored and mixture has doubled in volume. Remove bowl from heat; beat in lemon peel. Gradually fold in flour.
3. In a medium bowl, beat egg whites until stiff but not dry. Stir about 1/3 of beaten egg whites into egg-yolk mixture to lighten. Fold in remaining beaten egg whites. Fold in butter or margarine until no streaks remain. Pour mixture into prepared pan; smooth top.
4. Bake in preheated oven 25 to 30 minutes or until center springs back when lightly pressed. Cool in pan on a wire rack 10 minutes. Remove from pan; remove lining paper. Cool completely on wire rack. Use as directed in recipe. Makes 1 (10- or 11-inch) cake layer.

Basic Crepes

3/4 cup all-purpose flour
1/4 teaspoon salt
2 eggs
1 egg yolk
1/2 cup milk
1/2 cup water
2 tablespoons butter or margarine, melted
Butter or margarine

---

1. In a medium bowl, combine flour and salt. In a small bowl, beat eggs, egg yolk, milk and water until blended. Gradually stir egg mixture into flour mixture; beat with a whisk until smooth. Beat in 2 tablespoons butter or margarine until blended. Or combine crepe ingredients in a blender or food processor with a steel blade. Process 1 minute, scraping side of container once or twice. Process 15 to 20 seconds or until batter is smooth.
2. Pour batter into a pitcher. Cover and refrigerate 1 hour.
3. Cook crepes as directed above right for Dessert Crepes. To make ahead, place a small sheet of waxed paper between cooled, cooked crepes. Cooked crepes can be wrapped in foil and frozen up to 2 months. Thaw at room temperature about 1 hour before using. Makes 12 crepes.

Dessert Crepes

3/4 cup all-purpose flour
2 tablespoons sugar
1/2 teaspoon salt
3 eggs
1-1/2 cups milk or half and half
2 tablespoons butter or margarine, melted
2 tablespoons brandy or dark rum, if desired
1 teaspoon grated lemon peel or orange peel, if desired
Butter or margarine

---

1. In a medium bowl, combine flour, sugar and salt. In a small bowl, beat eggs and milk or half and half until blended. Gradually stir egg mixture into flour mixture; beat with a whisk until smooth. Beat in 2 tablespoons butter or margarine until blended. Stir in brandy or rum and lemon peel or orange peel, if desired. Or combine crepe ingredients in a blender or food processor with a steel blade. Process 1 minute, scraping side of container once or twice. Process 15 to 20 seconds or until batter is smooth.
2. Pour batter into a pitcher. Cover and refrigerate 1 hour.
3. To cook, melt 1 teaspoon butter or margarine in a 6- or 7-inch crepe pan over medium heat. Stir crepe batter. Pour 2 to 3 tablespoons batter, or enough batter to make a thin layer, into pan. Tilt pan from side to side to spread batter evenly. Cook 1 to 1-1/2 minutes.
4. Turn crepe; cook 1 to 1-1/2 minutes or until bottom is golden brown. Slide crepe onto a flat plate. Repeat with remaining batter to make 12 crepes, adding more butter or margarine to pan as necessary.
5. To make ahead, place a small sheet of waxed paper between cooled, cooked crepes. Cooked crepes can be wrapped in foil and frozen up to 2 months. Thaw at room temperature about 1 hour before using. Makes 12 crepes.

Special Cheesecakes

Mocha-Cheese Pie

Almond Pastry:
1-1/3 cups ground almonds
1/4 cup sugar
1 egg white

Filling:
1 cup half and half
6 oz. semisweet chocolate, chopped
1 (1/4-oz.) envelope unflavored gelatin (1 tablespoon)
1/4 cup water
1 (8-oz.) pkg. cream cheese, room temperature
2 tablespoons coffee liqueur

To decorate:
Sweetened whipped cream
Chocolate coffee-bean candies

1. To make pastry, in a medium bowl, knead almonds, sugar and egg white into a firm paste. Shape into a flattened ball. Wrap in plastic wrap; refrigerate 30 minutes.
2. Preheat oven to 350F (175C). Grease an 8-inch fluted quiche pan or tart pan with a removable bottom. Pat chilled pastry over bottom and up side of greased pan. Line pastry with foil; fill foil with pie weights or dried beans.
3. Bake in preheated oven 15 minutes. Remove foil and pie weights or beans. Bake 10 to 15 minutes more or until pastry is golden brown. Cool completely on a wire rack.
4. To make filling, in a heavy medium saucepan, combine half and half and chocolate. Stir over low heat until chocolate melts and mixture is smooth. Pour chocolate mixture into a medium bowl; refrigerate 30 minutes.
5. In a small saucepan, combine gelatin and water. Stir well; let stand 3 minutes. Stir over low heat until gelatin dissolves; cool to room temperature.
6. Beat chilled chocolate mixture until light. Beat in cream cheese and liqueur. Beat in cooled gelatin mixture until blended. Pour mixture into cooled pastry shell; smooth top. Refrigerate 3 to 4 hours or until set.
7. To serve, remove from pan; place on a serving dish. Decorate with swirls of sweetened whipped cream and coffee-bean candies. Makes 6 to 8 servings.

Crema di Mascarpone

1/2 cup raisins
5 tablespoons dark rum
2 tablespoons instant coffee powder
2 tablespoons boiling water
1 (8-oz.) pkg. cream cheese, room temperature
2 (3-oz.) pkgs. cream cheese, room temperature
1/2 cup dairy sour cream
3/4 cup sugar
4 egg yolks
2 egg whites
15 to 20 small almond macaroons

1. Lightly grease a 9" x 5" loaf pan. In a small bowl, combine raisins and rum; let stand 30 minutes. Drain, reserving rum. In a small bowl, dissolve coffee powder in boiling water.
2. In a medium bowl, beat cream cheese, sour cream, sugar and egg yolks until light and fluffy. Stir in 1 tablespoon dissolved coffee, soaked raisins and 3 tablespoons rum from raisins.
3. Line bottom of greased loaf pan with macaroons. Add remaining 2 tablespoons rum from raisins to remaining 1 tablespoon dissolved coffee; sprinkle over macaroons to moisten.
4. In a medium bowl, beat egg whites until stiff but not dry; fold beaten egg whites into cream-cheese mixture. Pour mixture over macaroons; smooth top. Cover and freeze 6 hours or until firm. Mixture can be frozen up to 1 month. If frozen hard, soften in refrigerator 1 hour before serving.
5. To serve, insert a knife inside of pan to loosen dessert. Invert on a serving plate. Remove pan. Makes about 6 servings.

Variation
For special occasions, serve Crema di Mascarpone with a chilled chocolate sauce. To make sauce, in a medium saucepan, combine 2 tablespoons unsweetend cocoa powder, 1/4 cup corn syrup, 1/4 cup butter, 1/2 cup milk and 1/2 teaspoon vanilla extract. Stir over medium heat; bring to a boil. Cook 2 to 3 minutes. Cool slightly; cover and refrigerate until chilled. To serve, spoon a little chocolate sauce into each serving dish. Add 1 tablespoon half and half to sauce, placing it off center. Draw a toothpick or fine skewer through half and half, feathering it into chocolate sauce. Carefully place a slice of frozen Crema di Mascarpone on each plate; serve immediately.

Top to bottom: Crema di Mascarpone, Mocha-Cheese Pie

Torta di Ricotta

1 lb. ricotta cheese (2 cups), drained
3/4 cup sugar
1/8 teaspoon almond extract
7 eggs, separated
1-1/4 cups ground almonds (about 6 oz.)
1 tablespoon grated orange peel
1/4 cup chopped candied orange peel
2 tablespoons cornstarch

To decorate:
Candied orange peel
Angelica pieces
Powdered sugar

1. Preheat oven to 350F (175C). Grease a 10-inch spring-form pan.
2. In a large bowl, beat ricotta cheese and sugar until creamy; beat in almond extract. Beat in egg yolks, 1 at a time, beating well after each addition. Beat in almonds, grated orange peel and candied orange peel.
3. In a medium bowl, beat egg whites until stiff but not dry; fold 1/2 of beaten egg whites into cheese mixture. Sift cornstarch over cheese mixture; fold in with remaining egg white. Pour mixture into greased pan; smooth top.
4. Bake in preheated oven 50 minutes or until golden brown and a wooden pick inserted off center comes out clean. Cool in pan on a wire rack.
5. Carefully remove side of pan; set cake on a serving plate. Refrigerate until served. Immediately before serving, sift powdered sugar over cake. Decorate with candied orange peel and angelica. Serve with Orange Sauce, below. Makes 10 to 12 servings.

Orange Sauce

Peel of 2 oranges, cut into julienne strips
3 tablespoons water
3/4 cup sugar
1/3 cup orange juice
1/4 cup lemon juice

1. In a medium saucepan, combine orange peel with enough boiling water to cover; simmer 6 minutes or until softened. Drain; set aside.
2. In a small saucepan over medium heat, combine 3 tablespoons water and sugar; bring to a boil, stirring. Stir in orange juice, lemon juice and blanched orange peel.
3. Reduce heat; simmer 20 minutes. Cool slightly. Refrigerate until chilled. Makes about 1 cup.

Italian Ricotta Cheesecake

Pastry:
2 cups all-purpose flour
1/4 cup sugar
1 teaspoon grated lemon peel
10 tablespoons butter or margarine, room temperature
2 egg yolks
2 tablespoons iced water
1 egg white
1 egg yolk beaten with 1 tablespoon milk for glaze

Filling:
5 egg yolks
1/4 cup granulated sugar
1 tablespoon cornstarch
2/3 cup milk
1 teaspoon vanilla extract
1-1/2 cups ricotta cheese, drained
1/2 cup powdered sugar
3 tablespoons all-purpose flour
2 tablespoons chopped citron
2 tablespoons chopped candied orange peel
2 tablespoons chopped candied lemon peel
2 tablespoons orange-flavored liqueur
3 egg whites

Left to right: Torta di Ricotta with Orange Sauce, Italian Ricotta Cheesecake

---

1. To make pastry, in a medium bowl, combine flour, sugar and lemon peel. Add butter or margarine, egg yolks and iced water. Work with your fingertips to make a smooth dough. Wrap dough in plastic wrap; refrigerate 30 minutes. Reserve egg white and egg-yolk glaze.

2. To make filling, in a medium saucepan, beat 2 egg yolks, granulated sugar and cornstarch until blended. Stir in milk until combined. Cook over low heat, stirring, until thickened. Do not boil. Remove from heat; stir in vanilla. Cover surface of custard with a sheet of waxed paper to prevent a skin from forming. Cool custard slightly.

3. In a medium bowl, beat ricotta cheese, remaining 3 egg yolks, powdered sugar and flour until blended. Fold in citron, orange peel, lemon peel and liqueur. Stir in cooled custard until combined; set aside.

4. Preheat oven to 375F (190C). Grease a 10-inch springform pan. Divide pastry into 2 pieces, making 1 piece 2/3 of pastry. On a lightly floured surface, roll or pat out large piece of pastry. Use pastry to line bottom and side of greased pan, pressing pastry about 1 inch up side of pan. Lightly beat reserved egg white. Brush pastry with beaten egg white. Roll out remaining pastry to 3/8 inch thick; cut 10 (1/4-inch) wide strips. Set pastry strips aside.

5. In a medium bowl, beat 3 egg whites until stiff but not dry. Fold beaten egg whites into cheese mixture. Pour into pastry-lined pan; smooth top. Arrange pastry strips in a lattice pattern over cheese filling. Brush pastry edge and strips with reserved egg-yolk glaze.

6. Bake in preheated oven 45 to 50 minutes or until a wooden pick inserted off center in filling comes out clean. Cool completely in pan on a wire rack. Refrigerate until served.

7. To serve, remove side of pan; place cheesecake on a serving plate. Sift powdered sugar over top. Makes 10 to 12 servings.

Apricot Cheesecake

Sour-Cream Pastry:
1/2 cup butter or margarine, room temperature
1/4 cup dairy sour cream
2 tablespoons sugar
1 egg yolk
1-1/2 cups sifted all-purpose flour

Filling:
2 tablespoons ground almonds
1 (29-oz.) can apricot halves, drained
1/4 cup butter or margarine, room temperature
1 (8-oz.) pkg. cream cheese, room temperature
2 eggs
1/4 cup sugar
1 teaspoon ground cinnamon
1/2 teaspoon grated lemon peel
1/2 cup dairy sour cream

To decorate:
Sweetened whipped cream
Toasted sliced almonds

1. To make pastry, in a medium bowl, beat butter or margarine, sour cream, sugar and egg yolk until blended. With a wooden spoon, stir in flour to make a smooth dough. Wrap dough in plastic wrap; refrigerate 30 minutes.
2. Preheat oven to 350F (175C). Grease a 9-inch springform pan. Pat dough over bottom and 1-1/2 inches up side of greased pan.
3. To fill, sprinkle ground almonds in bottom of pastry-lined pan. Set 4 apricot halves aside for decoration. Arrange remaining apricots, cut-side down, over almonds in pastry-lined pan.
4. In a medium bowl, beat butter or margarine, cream cheese, eggs and sugar until blended. Beat in cinnamon and lemon peel until combined. Fold in sour cream. Pour cream-cheese mixture over apricots; smooth top.
5. Bake in preheated oven 1 hour 10 minutes or until top is golden brown and a wooden pick inserted off center comes out clean. Cool completely in pan on a wire rack. Refrigerate until served.
6. To serve, remove side of pan; place cheesecake on a serving plate. Cut reserved apricots in half; arrange in a circle on top of cheesecake. Spoon whipped cream into a pastry bag fitted with a large star tip. Pipe whipped-cream rosettes around apricots. Top rosettes with sliced almonds. Makes 8 to 10 servings.

Fresh-Cranberry Cheesecake

1 (8-inch) Crumb Crust, page 7

Topping:
3 cups fresh cranberries
3 (2-inch) strips orange peel
2/3 cup sugar
3/4 cup water

Filling:
1 (1/4-oz.) envelope unflavored gelatin (1 tablespoon)
1/2 cup orange juice
1 (8-oz.) pkg. cream cheese, room temperature
1 cup small-curd cottage cheese
1 tablespoon grated orange peel
1/2 cup firmly packed light-brown sugar
3/4 cup whipping cream
1-1/2 tablespoons powdered sugar

To decorate:
Julienned orange peel

1. Grease an 8-inch springform pan. Press crust into bottom of greased pan.
2. To make topping, in a medium saucepan, combine cranberries, orange peel and sugar. Stir in water. Stir over medium heat; bring to a boil. Reduce heat; simmer 5 minutes or until skins begin to pop. Skim foam from surface. Let cool to room temperature.
3. To make filling, in a small saucepan, combine gelatin and orange juice. Stir well; let stand 3 minutes. Stir over low heat until gelatin dissolves; cool to room temperature.
4. In a medium bowl, beat cream cheese and cottage cheese until smooth. Beat in orange peel and brown sugar until blended. Gradually beat in cooled gelatin mixture.
5. In a medium bowl, beat cream until soft peaks form. Beat in powdered sugar. Spoon 1/2 cup whipped-cream mixture into a pastry bag fitted with medium star tip; refrigerate. Fold remaining whipped-cream mixture into cream-cheese mixture. Refrigerate mixture 20 to 30 minutes or until mixture mounds when dropped from a spoon.
6. Drain reserved cranberry mixture, discarding juice and strips of orange peel. Spread 1/2 of drained cranberries over crumb crust in pan. Cover and refrigerate remaining cranberries. Spoon filling over cranberries; smooth top. Refrigerate several hours or until served.
7. To serve, run a knife around edge of cheesecake; remove side of pan. Place cheesecake on a serving plate. Spoon reserved cranberries over top. Pipe chilled whipped-cream mixture in rosettes on top of cranberries. Decorate with strips of orange peel. Makes 8 servings.

Blackberry & Cheese Torte

1 recipe Sweet Shortcrust Pastry, page 8
1 egg white, beaten

Filling:
2 cups blackberries, thawed, if frozen
1/2 cup sugar
2/3 cup coarsely crushed macaroons
1 (8-oz.) pkg. cream cheese, room temperature
2 tablespoons kirsch
3 tablespoons whipping cream
2 egg yolks
1 egg white

To decorate:
Whipped cream

1. Grease an 8-inch springform pan. Prepare pastry as directed on page 8. Bake blind as directed on page 8.

2. Preheat oven to 375F (190C). To make filling, reserve 1/4 cup blackberries in a small bowl for decoration. Cover and refrigerate. In a medium bowl, combine remaining blackberries and 1/4 cup sugar.
3. Scatter 1/2 of macaroons over cooled pastry shell; spoon sugared blackberries over macaroons.
4. In a medium bowl, beat cream cheese, kirsch, whipping cream, egg yolks and remaining 1/4 cup sugar until smooth. In a small bowl, beat egg white until stiff but not dry; fold into cream-cheese mixture. Pour mixture into pan; scatter remaining macaroons on top.
5. Bake in preheated oven 45 minutes or until a wooden pick inserted off center comes out clean. Cool in pan on a wire rack.
6. Refrigerate until served. To serve, carefully remove side of pan; place torte on a serving plate. Spoon whipped cream into a pastry bag fitted with a large star tip. Pipe swirls of whipped cream around center of cheesecake. Fill center with reserved blackberries. Makes 8 servings.

Clockwise from top left: Fresh-Cranberry Cheesecake, Blackberry & Cheese Torte, Apricot Cheesecake

Tart Lemon Cheesecake

1 (8-inch) Crumb Crust, page 7
Filling:
4 eggs, separated
1-1/4 cups sugar
2/3 cup water
2 (1/4-oz.) envelopes unflavored gelatin (2 tablespoons)
3/4 cup lemon juice
4 teaspoons grated lemon peel
1-1/2 cups small-curd cottage cheese, drained

To decorate:
Sweetened whipped cream
Lemon slices, quartered
Seedless grapes, halved

---

1. Grease an 8-inch springform pan. Press crust into bottom of pan. Refrigerate 30 minutes.
2. To make filling, in a large bowl, beat egg yolks until thick and lemon-colored.
3. In a small saucepan, combine sugar and 1/3 cup water. Stir over medium heat until sugar dissolves; bring to a boil, stirring to dissolve sugar. Boil rapidly to soft-ball stage 235F (115C) on a candy thermometer.
4. Pour sugar syrup in a slow steady stream into beaten egg yolks, beating constantly. Continue beating until mixture is cool.
5. In a small saucepan, combine gelatin and remaining 1/3 cup water. Stir well; let stand 3 minutes. Stir over low heat until gelatin dissolves; cool to room temperature. Stir cooled gelatin, lemon juice and lemon peel into beaten egg-yolk mixture; set aside.
6. In a blender or food processor with a steel blade, process cottage cheese until smooth. Fold processed cottage cheese into egg-yolk mixture. Refrigerate until mixture mounds when dropped from a spoon.
7. In a medium bowl, beat egg whites until stiff but not dry. Fold beaten egg whites into cottage-cheese mixture. Pour mixture into crust-lined pan; smooth top. Refrigerate 3 to 4 hours or until set.
8. To serve, run a knife around inside edge of pan; carefully release side of pan. Place cheesecake on a serving plate. Spoon whipped cream into a pastry bag fitted with a large star tip. Pipe swirls of whipped cream in a circle on cheesecake. Decorate with lemon slices and grapes. Makes 8 to 10 servings.

Pineapple Refrigerator Cake

1 (9-inch) Nut-Crumb Crust, page 7
Filling:
1 (8-oz.) can crushed pineapple, juice pack
2 (1/4-oz.) envelopes unflavored gelatin (2 tablespoons)
3/4 cup sugar
Pinch of salt
3 eggs, separated
1 cup milk
2-1/2 (8-oz.) pkgs. Neufchâtel cheese, room temperature
2 teaspoons grated lemon peel
3 tablespoons lemon juice
1/2 pint whipping cream (1 cup)

To decorate:
1/2 cup dairy sour cream
Candied pineapple
1/4 cup toasted sliced almonds
Geranium leaves, if desired

---

1. Grease a 9-inch springform pan. Press crust into bottom of greased pan. Refrigerate while preparing filling.
2. Drain pineapple, pouring juice into top of a double boiler. Stir in gelatin. Let stand 3 minutes. Stir in sugar and salt. Beat in egg yolks and milk. Stir in pineapple.
3. Cook, stirring, over a pan of simmering water about 15 minutes or until mixture starts to thicken. Pour gelatin mixture into a large bowl. Cool to room temperature.
4. In a large bowl, beat cheese, lemon peel and lemon juice. Gradually stir in cooled pineapple mixture until combined. Refrigerate about 15 minutes or until mixture mounds when dropped from a spoon.
5. In a medium bowl, beat whipping cream until soft peaks form. Fold whipped cream into pineapple mixture. In a medium bowl, beat egg whites until stiff but not dry. Fold beaten egg whites into pineapple mixture. Pour mixture into prepared pan; smooth top. Refrigerate until set.
6. To serve, run a knife around inside edge of pan. Carefully release side of pan; place cheesecake on a serving plate. Spread sour cream over surface; decorate with candied pineapple and toasted almonds. Arrange geranium leaves in center, if desired. Makes 12 servings.

Top to bottom: Pineapple Refrigerator Cake, Tart Lemon Cheesecake

Mocha-Rum Cheesecake

1 (10-inch) Nut-Crumb Crust, page 7

Filling:
2 tablespoons instant coffee powder
3 tablespoons boiling water
4 oz. semisweet chocolate, chopped
2 tablespoons dark rum
3/4 cup plus 2 tablespoons sugar
1 (1/4-oz.) envelope plus 1 teaspoon unflavored gelatin
1/3 cup milk
2 (8-oz.) pkgs. cream cheese, room temperature
4 eggs, separated
1-1/2 cups whipping cream
1/3 cup finely chopped walnuts or pecans

To decorate:
Walnut halves
Chocolate curls
Powdered sugar

1. Grease bottom and side of a 10-inch springform pan. Press crust into bottom of greased pan.
2. In a small heavy saucepan over low heat, stir coffee, hot water and chocolate until smooth. Stir in rum and 2 tablespoons sugar. Cool slightly.
3. In a small saucepan, combine gelatin and milk. Stir well; let stand 3 minutes. Stir over low heat until gelatin dissolves; cool to room temperature.
4. In a large bowl, beat cream cheese, remaining 3/4 cup sugar and egg yolks until blended. Gradually beat in cooled gelatin.
5. In a medium bowl, beat cream until soft peaks form. Fold whipped cream into cheese mixture. In a medium bowl, beat egg whites until stiff but not dry. Fold in beaten egg whites.
6. Spoon 1/3 of cheese mixture into a small bowl. Fold in cooled chocolate mixture. Fold walnuts or pecans into remaining plain cheese mixture.
7. Spoon nut-cheese mixture into crust-lined pan; smooth top. Spoon chocolate-cheese mixture in mounds on top of nut-cheese mixture. Gently swirl through both mixtures with a small spatula. Refrigerate several hours or until served.
8. To serve, run a knife around inside edge of pan. Remove side of pan; place cheesecake on a serving plate. Decorate with walnut halves and chocolate curls. Dust chocolate curls lightly with powdered sugar. Makes 10 to 12 servings.

Cassata alla Siciliana

1 baked Genoise Sponge, page 11, or 1 pound cake, cut into 1/2-inch slices

Filling:
1/4 cup Maraschino liqueur or Grand Marnier
1 lb. ricotta cheese (2 cups), drained
1 cup half and half
1/3 cup sugar
1 teaspoon ground cinnamon
4 oz. semisweet chocolate, finely chopped
1/2 cup chopped mixed candied fruit
1/4 cup chopped pistachios or almonds
1/2 teaspoon orange-flower water

Icing:
1 tablespoon lemon juice
1-1/3 cups powdered sugar, sifted
About 3 tablespoons hot water

To decorate:
Assorted whole candied fruit, if desired

1. Line bottom and side of a 1-1/2-quart charlotte mold or a deep 7-inch cake pan with waxed paper.
2. Use 3/4 of cake slices to line bottom and side of container, cutting and trimming to fit; see below. Sprinkle 2 tablespoons liqueur over cake.
3. To make filling, in a blender or food processor with a steel blade, process ricotta cheese until smooth. Spoon into a bowl; beat in half and half, sugar, cinnamon, chocolate, candied fruit and nuts. Stir in orange-flower water. Pour into prepared mold or pan; smooth top. Trim remaining cake slices; arrange over filling. Sprinkle cake with remaining liqueur. Cover and refrigerate 3 to 4 hours.
4. Carefully unmold cake onto a serving plate; remove mold or pan and waxed paper.
5. To make icing, in a small bowl, combine lemon juice and powdered sugar. Stir in water, 1 tablespoon at a time, until icing is a good consistency for pouring. Pour icing over cake, letting it come part way down side. Smooth with a small spatula, if necessary.
6. While icing is soft, decorate with candied fruit, if desired. Refrigerate up to 1 day or until served. Makes 12 servings.

 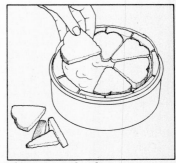

1/Trim cake slices to fit pan. 2/Arrange cake slices over filling.

Hungarian Hot-Crepe Gâteau

1 (8-oz.) pkg. cream cheese, room temperature
1 (3-oz.) pkg. cream cheese, room temperature
3 eggs, separated
2/3 cup sugar
2 tablespoons grated lemon peel
3/4 cup chopped walnuts, ground
1 tablespoon grated orange peel
12 Dessert Crepes, page 11

To decorate:
Coarsely chopped walnuts

Filled and rolled crepes are a well-known dessert, but this layered cheesecake is an unusual variation.

1. Preheat oven to 425F (220C). Grease a 7- or 8-inch springform pan. In a medium bowl, beat cream cheese, egg yolks, sugar and lemon peel until combined. Stir in walnuts and orange peel. In a medium bowl, beat egg whites until stiff but not dry. Fold in beaten egg whites.
2. Place 1 crepe in greased pan. Spread with 1-1/2 tablespoons filling. Repeat layers of crepes and filling, ending with a crepe.
3. Bake in preheated oven 10 to 15 minutes or until heated through.
4. To serve, carefully remove side of pan; place gâteau on a serving plate. Sprinkle chopped walnuts over gâteau. Cut in wedges; serve warm. Makes 6 servings.

Left to right: Mocha-Rum Cheesecake, Cassata alla Siciliana

Cherry Cheesecake

1 (16-oz.) jar pitted dark sweet cherries
1 (1/4-oz.) envelope unflavored gelatin (1 tablespoon)
1/4 cup milk
1/4 cup butter or margarine, room temperature
1 cup sugar
2 eggs, separated
2 (7-1/2-oz.) pkgs. farmer's cheese, drained
2 teaspoons grated lemon peel
2 tablespoons lemon juice
3/4 cup whipping cream
6 tablespoons kirsch
1 baked Genoise Sponge, page 11
1/3 cup toasted sliced almonds

To decorate:
Fresh cherries
Angelica pieces

Kirsch is an eau-de-vie distilled from cherries. Its traditional combination with chocolate cake, dark cherries and cream originates in the Black Forest of Germany. This cheesecake is an unusual variation. For a more authentic version, use a chocolate sponge cake; see variation, page 10.

1. Drain cherries, reserving 3 tablespoons syrup. Coarsely chop drained cherries; set aside. Grease bottom and side of a 10-inch springform pan.
2. In a small saucepan, combine gelatin and milk. Stir well; let stand 3 minutes. Stir over low heat until gelatin dissolves; cool to room temperature.
3. In a large bowl, beat butter or margarine and sugar until light and fluffy. Beat in egg yolks, farmer's cheese, lemon peel and lemon juice until blended. Gradually beat in cooled gelatin mixture until blended. Refrigerate 20 to 30 minutes or until mixture mounds when dropped from a spoon.
4. In a medium bowl, beat cream until soft peaks form. Fold whipped cream into cheese mixture. In a medium bowl, beat egg whites until stiff but not dry. Fold beaten egg whites into cheese mixture. Fold in 3 tablespoons kirsch.
5. Place cake in bottom of greased springform pan. Combine remaining 3 tablespoons kirsch and reserved 3 tablespoons cherry syrup; sprinkle over cake. Sprinkle almonds over cake. Spoon 1/2 of chopped cherries over cake. Fold remaining cherries into cheese mixture. Spoon cheese mixture over sponge cake; smooth top. Refrigerate 4 to 5 hours or until set.
6. To serve, run a knife around inside edge of pan. Carefully remove side of pan. Place on a serving plate. Decorate top with fresh cherries and angelica. Makes 10 to 12 servings.

Green-Grape Cheesecake

1 Sweet Shortcrust Pastry, page 8
Filling:
1 tablespoon butter or margarine, melted
2 cups seedless green grapes, halved
1/4 cup butter or margarine, room temperature
2/3 cup sugar
3 eggs, separated
1 teaspoon grated lemon peel
2 tablespoons whipping cream
2 tablespoons kirsch
2 (8-oz.) pkgs. cream cheese, room temperature
3 tablespoons cornstarch

Topping:
1 egg yolk
2 tablespoons whipping cream
2 teaspoons sugar
2 tablespoons sliced almonds

To decorate:
Powdered sugar
Whole green grapes

---

1. Preheat oven to 400F (205C). Grease a 9-inch springform pan. Prepare pastry as directed on page 8. Bake blind as directed on page 8.
2. Preheat oven to 375F (190C). To fill pastry, brush bottom of pastry with melted butter or margarine; arrange halved grapes on buttered pastry.
3. In a medium bowl, beat 1/4 cup butter or margarine and sugar until smooth. Beat in egg yolks until light and fluffy. Beat in lemon peel, whipping cream, kirsch, cream cheese and cornstarch until blended.
4. In a medium bowl, beat egg whites until stiff but not dry; fold beaten egg whites into cream-cheese mixture. Pour mixture over grapes; smooth top.
5. To make topping, in a small bowl, combine egg yolk, whipping cream and sugar; spread over filling. Sprinkle with almonds.
6. Bake in preheated oven 1-1/4 hours or until golden brown and a wooden pick inserted off center comes out clean. Cool in pan on a wire rack 30 minutes. Refrigerate until served.
7. To serve, carefully remove side of pan. Place cheesecake on a serving plate. Arrange whole grapes on top; sift powdered sugar over top. Makes 10 servings.

Variations
Substitute any firm fresh fruit for grapes. Try pitted sweet cherries, halved plums or sliced apples or pears. Toss sliced fruit for decoration in lemon juice before using.

Left to right: Green-Grape Cheesecake, Cherry Cheesecake

Apple & Cheese Soufflé Cake

1 (8-inch) Crumb Crust, page 7

Filling:
1 lb. tart apples (about 3 apples), peeled, sliced
2 tablespoons lemon juice
Powdered sugar
4 eggs, separated
2/3 cup granulated sugar
1 lb. ricotta cheese or small-curd cottage cheese (2 cups), drained
1 tablespoon grated lemon peel
1/2 cup all-purpose flour
1 teaspoon baking powder

---

1. Preheat oven to 350F (175C). Grease an 8-inch spring-form pan. Line side of pan with parchment paper, extending paper 2 inches above rim of pan. Fasten parchment collar with tape. Press crust onto unlined bottom of pan.
2. To make filling, in a medium bowl, combine apples, lemon juice and 2 tablespoons powdered sugar. Arrange apple slices on crumb crust in pan. Set aside.
3. In a medium bowl, beat egg yolks and granulated sugar until thick and lemon-colored. Beat in ricotta cheese or cottage cheese and lemon peel until mixture is smooth. Sift flour and baking powder over cheese mixture; fold in. In a medium bowl, beat egg whites until stiff but not dry; fold beaten egg whites into cheese mixture. Pour cheese mixture over apples; smooth top.
4. Bake in preheated oven 1 hour 15 minutes or until center is set and top is golden brown. Cool in pan on a wire rack 30 minutes. Remove side of pan; carefully remove parchment collar. Place cake on a serving plate; dust top with powdered sugar. Serve warm or refrigerate until served. Makes 8 to 10 servings.

Raisin-Cinnamon Cheesecake

1 recipe Yeast Dough, page 9

Filling:
3 egg yolks
1/3 cup sugar
1-1/2 (8-oz.) pkgs. cream cheese, room temperature
1/2 teaspoon ground cinnamon
1/4 cup whipping cream
2 tablespoons all-purpose flour
3 tablespoons ground almonds
1/3 cup golden raisins
1 tablespoon butter or margarine, melted
2 tablespoons dry bread crumbs
1 egg yolk beaten with 1 tablespoon milk for glaze

---

1. Grease a 10-inch springform pan.
2. Prepare dough as directed on page 9 through step 5. Divide dough into 2 pieces, making 1 piece 2/3 of dough. Cover and refrigerate small piece of dough. On a lightly floured surface, roll out remaining piece of dough into a 12-inch circle.
3. Use dough to line greased pan, pressing dough 1 inch up side of pan. Cover pan with a towel. Let rise in a warm place, free from drafts, 20 minutes.
4. Preheat oven to 375F (190C). To make filling, in a medium bowl, beat egg yolks, sugar, cream cheese and cinnamon until blended. Beat in whipping cream. Sprinkle flour over cheese mixture; beat in. Fold in ground almonds and raisins.
5. Brush dough in pan with butter or margarine; sprinkle with bread crumbs. Spoon cheese filling into pan; smooth top.
6. Roll out refrigerated dough to 3/8 inch thick. Cut into 10 (1/4-inch) wide strips. Brush edge of filled dough with egg glaze. Arrange dough strips in a lattice pattern over cheese filling. Press to seal. Brush dough strips with egg glaze.
7. Bake in preheated oven 20 minutes. Reduce oven temperature to 350F (175C). Bake 25 to 30 minutes more or until a wooden pick inserted in filling comes out clean.
8. Cool in pan on a wire rack 10 minutes. Remove side of pan; cool completely on wire rack. Place on a serving plate. Refrigerate until served. Makes 10 to 12 servings.

Left to right: Raisin-Cinnamon Cheesecake, Apple & Cheese
Soufflé Cake

Lemon Cheesecake

1 (8-inch) Crumb-Nut Crust, page 7

Filling:
2 tablespoons grated lemon peel
3/4 cup lemon juice
2/3 cup firmly packed light-brown sugar
1 (8-oz.) pkg. cream cheese, room temperature
1 (3-oz.) pkg. cream cheese, room temperature
1-1/2 cups cottage cheese, sieved, drained
1/2 cup mixed candied orange peel and candied
  lemon peel
1/2 pint whipping cream (1 cup), whipped

To decorate:
Lemon slices

This chilled cheesecake has a thick mousse-like texture.

1. Grease an 8-inch springform pan. Press crust into bottom of pan.
2. To make filling, in a medium bowl, combine lemon peel, lemon juice and brown sugar. Beat in cheeses and candied peel until combined. Fold in whipped cream.
3. Pour filling over crust in pan; smooth top. Refrigerate 5 to 6 hours or until served.
4. To serve, run a knife around edge of cheesecake. Carefully remove side of pan; place cheesecake on a serving plate. Decorate with lemon slices. Makes 8 servings.

Cheesecakes for Entertaining

Austrian Baked Cheesecake

1/2 cup butter or margarine, room temperature
1/2 cup sugar
4 eggs, separated
1 teaspoon grated lemon peel
1/2 (8-oz.) pkg. cream cheese, room temperature
1 cup ground almonds (about 4 oz.)

To decorate:
Powdered sugar

This cake will rise very high during cooking and deflate dramatically as it cools. It still tastes very good!

1. Preheat oven to 350F (175C). Grease a 10-inch spring-form pan. Dust greased pan with flour; shake out excess flour. In a medium bowl, beat butter or margarine until light and fluffy. Beat in sugar and egg yolks, 1 at a time, beating well after each addition. Beat in lemon peel, cream cheese and almonds.
2. In a medium bowl, beat egg whites until stiff but not dry. Fold in beaten egg whites.
3. Pour mixture into prepared pan. Smooth top.
4. Bake in preheated oven 45 minutes or until golden brown and a wooden pick inserted off center comes out clean. Cool in pan on a wire rack.
5. Refrigerate until served. Carefully remove side of pan; place cheesecake on a serving plate. Immediately before serving, place a paper doily on top of cake; sift powdered sugar over doily. Carefully remove doily without disturbing pattern. Makes 6 to 8 servings.

Lemon Curd

Lemon curd is a delicious, thick lemon custard. It is traditionally eaten like jam in England. It is available in jars in the imported food section in supermarkets or gourmet stores.

Seventeenth-Century Cheese Tart

Filling:
1/2 pint whipping cream (1 cup)
1/4 cup sherry
3 eggs
2 egg yolks
1/4 cup sugar
2 tablespoons rose water
1/4 teaspoon ground mace
1/4 teaspoon ground cinnamon
1/4 teaspoon ground nutmeg
1/2 teaspoon salt
2 (3-oz.) pkgs. cream cheese, room temperature
1/3 cup currants

Crust:
1 recipe Shortcrust Pastry, page 8, baked blind in an 8-inch springform pan

To decorate:
Powdered sugar
Crystallized flower petals

Sift powdered sugar over cheesecake immediately before serving to prevent sugar soaking into surface of cheesecake.

1. To make filling, in a small saucepan over low heat, combine whipping cream and sherry. Heat to simmering. Remove from heat.
2. In a medium bowl, beat eggs, egg yolks, sugar, rose water, mace, cinnamon, nutmeg and salt until blended. Beat in cream cheese. Slowly pour whipping-cream mixture into cream-cheese mixture, beating constantly. Stir in currants. Pour mixture into pastry shell; smooth top.
3. Bake in preheated oven 1 hour or until a wooden pick inserted off center comes out clean.
4. Cool completely in pan on a wire rack. Refrigerate until served.
5. To serve, carefully remove side of pan; place cake on a serving plate. Immediately before serving, sift powdered sugar over cake. Decorate with flower petals. Makes 8 servings.

Left to right: Austrian Baked Cheesecake, Seventeenth-Century Cheese Tart

Cheese & Jam Tart

1-1/2 recipes Shortcrust Pastry, page 8
Filling:
1 egg
1 (8-oz.) pkg. cream cheese, room temperature
3 tablespoons sugar
1 cup seedless raspberry jam

This tart is best if eaten the same day it is made.

1. Preheat oven to 350F (175C). Lightly grease a 10-inch tart pan with removable bottom.

2. Prepare pastry as directed on page 8. Divide dough into 2 pieces, making 1 piece 2/3 of dough. On a lightly floured surface, roll out large piece of dough to a 13-inch circle. Use pastry to line greased pan. Set remaining pastry aside.

3. To make filling, in a medium bowl, beat egg, cream cheese and sugar until light and fluffy. Spread cream-cheese mixture over bottom of pastry. Spread jam over cream-cheese mixture.

4. Roll out remaining pastry to about 1/8 inch thick. Cut into long 1/2-inch-wide strips. Brush edge of pastry shell with water. Lay strips over filling in a lattice pattern. Press edges to pastry shell to seal; trim even with pan.

5. Bake in preheated oven 40 minutes or until pastry is golden brown. Cool on a wire rack 15 minutes.

6. Remove from pan. Place on a serving plate. Serve warm or refrigerate until served. Makes 8 servings.

Left to right: Cheese & Jam Tart, Ginger & Cheese Tarts

Ginger & Cheese Tarts

12 baked Sweet Shortcrust Tarts, page 8
Filling:
1 (8-oz.) pkg. cream cheese, room temperature
1/3 cup sugar
2 eggs
1 teaspoon grated lemon peel
1-1/2 teaspoons ground ginger
3 tablespoons currants
2 tablespoons whipping cream

1. Preheat oven to 375F (190C).
2. To make filling, in a medium bowl, beat cream cheese and sugar until light and fluffy. Beat in eggs, 1 at a time, beating well after each addition. Beat in lemon peel and ground ginger until blended. Stir in currants and whipping cream. Spoon filling into cooled tart shells, filling shells 1/2 to 2/3 full.
3. Bake in preheated oven 25 to 30 minutes or until golden brown and a wooden pick inserted off center of tarts comes out clean. Cool in pans on wire racks. Remove from pans. Serve warm or refrigerate until served. Makes 12 tarts.

Cheese & Almond Cake

1-1/2 (8-oz.) pkgs. cream cheese, room temperature
1/2 cup sugar
2 egg yolks
2 teaspoons grated lemon peel
1 tablespoon cornstarch
1 tablespoon all-purpose flour
1/3 cup raisins
1-1/3 cups sliced almonds
4 egg whites

To decorate:
2 tablespoons powdered sugar

1. Preheat oven to 450F (230C). Grease a 9-inch springform pan.
2. In a medium bowl, beat cream cheese and sugar until light and fluffy. Beat in egg yolks, 1 at a time, beating well after each addition. Beat in lemon peel.
3. Sift cornstarch and flour over cheese mixture; stir in. Beat in raisins until distributed. Reserve 2 tablespoons almonds; fold remaining almonds into mixture.
4. In a medium bowl, beat egg whites until stiff but not dry; fold beaten egg whites into mixture.
5. Pour mixture into greased pan; smooth top. Sprinkle with reserved almonds.
6. Place in preheated oven; immediately reduce oven temperature to 325F (165C). Bake 40 to 45 minutes or until puffed and golden brown. *Do not open oven door* to check cake until 40 minutes are up or it will collapse. Cool in pan on a wire rack.
7. Immediately before serving, sift powdered sugar over cheesecake. Refrigerate until served or up to 2 days. Makes 6 servings.

Fresh-Grape Cheesecake

1 recipe Sweet Shortcrust Pastry, page 8

Filling:
1 lb. seedless red grapes, halved
1 tablespoon lemon juice
3/4 cup sugar
1 lb. ricotta cheese (2 cups), drained
3 eggs, separated
1 tablespoon grated lemon peel
1/2 cup all-purpose flour
1 teaspoon baking powder

To decorate:
Sweetened whipped cream
Red-grape halves

1. Preheat oven to 350F (175C). Grease a 9-inch springform pan. Prepare pastry as directed on page 8. Press pastry over bottom and 1 inch up side of greased pan.

2. To make filling, in a medium bowl, combine grapes, lemon juice and 1/4 cup sugar. Toss gently; set aside.

3. In a medium bowl, beat ricotta cheese and remaining 1/2 cup sugar until blended. Beat in egg yolks, 1 at a time, beating well after each addition. Beat in lemon peel. Sift flour and baking powder over cheese mixture; beat until blended.

4. In a medium bowl, beat egg whites until stiff but not dry. Fold beaten egg whites into cheese mixture. Fold in grape mixture. Pour cheese mixture into pastry-lined pan; smooth top.

5. Bake in preheated oven 60 to 65 minutes or until a wooden pick inserted off center comes out clean. Cool completely in pan on a wire rack.

6. Refrigerate until served. To serve, carefully remove side of pan; place cheesecake on a serving plate. Spoon whipped cream into a pastry bag fitted with a large star tip. Pipe swirls of whipped cream around top edge of cheesecake. Arrange grape halves in cream. Makes 10 to 12 servings.

Strawberry Sour-Cream Cheesecake

1 (9- or 10-inch) Crumb Crust, page 7

Filling:
1-1/2 pints strawberries (3 cups)
3 tablespoons orange-flavored liqueur
1 (1/4-oz.) envelope plus 1 teaspoon unflavored gelatin
1/4 cup orange juice
2 (8-oz.) pkgs. cream cheese, room temperature
1 cup sugar
3 eggs, separated
2 teaspoons grated orange peel
1/2 pint dairy sour cream (1 cup)

To decorate:
1/2 pint whipping cream (1 cup)
2 tablespoons powdered sugar
Toasted sliced almonds

1. Grease a 9- or 10-inch springform pan. Refrigerate crust 30 minutes.
2. To make filling, set aside about 16 strawberries for decoration. In a blender or food processor with a steel blade, process remaining strawberries and liqueur until pureed. Pour strawberry puree into a medium bowl; set aside.
3. In a small saucepan, combine gelatin and orange juice. Stir well; let stand 3 minutes. Stir over low heat until gelatin dissolves. Cool to room temperature.
4. In a large bowl, beat cream cheese and sugar until light and fluffy. Beat in egg yolks, 1 at a time, beating well after each addition. Beat in strawberry puree and orange peel until blended.
5. Gradually beat in cooled gelatin mixture. Fold in sour cream. Refrigerate 20 minutes or until mixture mounds when dropped from a spoon.
6. In a medium bowl, beat egg whites until stiff but not dry. Fold beaten egg whites into cream-cheese mixture. Pour cream-cheese mixture over crust in pan; smooth top. Refrigerate several hours or until set.
7. To decorate, run a knife around inside edge of pan. Remove side of pan. Place on a serving plate.
8. To decorate, in a medium bowl, beat cream until soft peaks form. Beat in powdered sugar. Spoon 1 cup whipped cream into a pastry bag fitted with a medium open-star tip; refrigerate.
9. Spread remaining whipped-cream mixture over top of cheesecake; smooth with a long spatula. Pipe reserved whipped cream in scrolls in a circular pattern around center of cheesecake.
10. Thinly slice 8 to 10 strawberries; arrange slices around top edge of cheesecake, using only center slices. Place remaining strawberries in center of whipped-cream circle; decorate with sliced almonds. Refrigerate until served. Makes 10 to 12 servings.

Quince Cheesecake

Filling:
1 lb. fresh quinces
2-1/2 tablespoons lemon juice
2/3 cup sugar
1-1/2 cups water
1 recipe Sour-Cream Filling, from Easy Cheesecake, page 35
1/4 cup sugar

Crust:
1 Sweet Shortcrust Pastry, page 8, baked blind in a 9-inch springform pan

The edible quince is not to be confused with the hard, small fruits of spring-flowering japonica. Quinces look like a large pear. Their yellow flesh turns a deep pink when cooked. They have a strong sweet perfume and flavor. Quinces are available in autumn. If quinces are not available, substitute apples.

1. To make filling, peel, core and slice quinces, reserving peel and cores. Place quince slices in a large bowl. Cover with water; add 1/2 tablespoon lemon juice. Set aside.
2. In a large saucepan, combine quince trimmings, remaining 2 tablespoons lemon juice, 2/3 cup sugar and 1-1/2 cups water. Boil 30 minutes or until thick and syrupy. Strain syrup. Clean and dry pan. Pour syrup into clean pan.
3. Drain quince slices; add to syrup. Poach in syrup 30 minutes or until tender but not mushy. Drain, discarding syrup; cool poached slices to room temperature.
4. Preheat oven to 350F (175C). Prepare filling as directed on page 35. Arrange cooled quince slices over pastry shell in pan. Sprinkle with 1/4 cup sugar. Pour filling over quince slices.
5. Bake in preheated oven 50 minutes or until golden brown and a wooden pick inserted off center comes out clean. Cool in pan on a wire rack.
6. Refrigerate until served. To serve, carefully remove side of pan. Place cake on a serving plate. Makes 10 servings.

Custard-Cheese Tarts

1/3 cup sugar
1 tablespoon cornstarch
1/2 cup milk
2 egg yolks
1/2 teaspoon vanilla extract
2 tablespoons dark rum
1/4 cup butter or margarine, room temperature
1 cup ricotta cheese, drained
12 baked Sweet Shortcrust Tarts, page 8

To decorate:
Pieces of angelica or halved candied cherries

---

1. In a medium saucepan, combine sugar and cornstarch. In a small bowl, beat milk and egg yolks until blended. With a whisk, gradually beat milk mixture into sugar mixture until blended.
2. Cook over low heat, stirring constantly, until mixture thickens. Do not boil. Pour custard into a medium bowl. Stir in vanilla and rum. Cover surface of custard with a sheet of waxed paper to prevent a skin from forming. Refrigerate until chilled.
3. In a medium bowl, beat butter or margarine until light and fluffy. Beat in ricotta cheese until mixture is smooth. Gradually beat in chilled custard until blended.
4. Spoon cheese mixture into baked tart shells. Decorate each tart with angelica or candied-cherry halves. Refrigerate until served. Makes 12 tarts.

Maids of Honor

1 recipe Sweet Shortcrust Pastry, page 8
Filling:
1/2 (8-oz.) pkg. cream cheese, room temperature
6 tablespoons butter or margarine, room temperature
2 egg yolks
2 tablespoons brandy
1/2 cup sugar
3/4 cup ground almonds
Pinch of grated nutmeg
1 tablespoon lemon juice
1 teaspoon grated lemon peel

---

1. Prepare pastry as directed on page 8. Prepare tart shells. Bake as directed on page 8.
2. Preheat oven to 400F (205C).

3. To make filling, in a medium bowl, beat cream cheese and butter or margarine until smooth. Beat in egg yolks, 1 at a time, beating well after each addition. Beat in brandy, sugar and almonds until combined. Beat in nutmeg, lemon juice and lemon peel. Spoon mixture into pastry-lined pans.
4. Bake in preheated oven 25 minutes or until puffed and golden brown. Cool in pans on a wire rack. Refrigerate until served. Remove from pans. Makes 12 tarts.

Greek Honey Cheesecake

1 recipe Sweet Shortcrust Pastry, page 8

Filling:
1 (8-oz.) pkg. cream cheese, room temperature
1/2 pint whipping cream (1 cup)
1/4 cup honey
3 tablespoons sugar
1 teaspoon ground cinnamon
2 teaspoons grated lemon peel
1/2 teaspoon ground nutmeg
2 eggs, beaten

To decorate:
Whipped cream
Lemon slices, quartered

---

1. Preheat oven to 350F (175C). Grease an 8-inch springform pan.
2. Prepare pastry as directed on page 8. On a lightly floured surface, roll out pastry to a 10-inch circle. Use pastry to line greased pan, pressing pastry 1 inch up side.
3. To make filling, in a medium bowl, beat cream cheese and whipping cream until smooth. Beat in honey, 2 tablespoons sugar, 1/2 teaspoon cinnamon, lemon peel and nutmeg. Beat in eggs, 1 at a time, beating well after each addition.
4. Pour mixture into pastry-lined pan. In a small bowl, combine remaining 1 tablespoon sugar and 1/2 teaspoon cinnamon; sprinkle over filling.
5. Bake in preheated oven 1 hour or until filling puffs and pastry is golden brown. Cool in pan on a wire rack.
6. Refrigerate until served. Carefully remove side of pan; place cake on a serving plate. Spoon whipped cream into a pastry bag fitted with a star tip. Pipe rosettes of whipped cream around top of cheesecake. Place a lemon-slice quarter on each rosette. Makes 8 servings.

Left to right: Custard-Cheese Tarts, Greek Honey Cheesecake

Cream-Cheese & Nut-Filled Pastry

Pastry:
2 (3-oz.) pkgs. cream cheese, room temperature
1/3 cup butter or margarine, room temperature
1/4 cup sugar
6 tablespoons milk
2-1/4 cups sifted all-purpose flour
1 teaspoon baking powder
1 egg yolk beaten with 1 tablespoon milk for glaze

Filling:
1/4 cup butter or margarine, room temperature
1/3 cup sugar
1 (8-oz.) pkg. cream cheese, room temperature
1 teaspoon vanilla extract
1/3 cup finely ground hazelnuts or almonds
1/3 cup golden raisins

To decorate:
Powdered sugar

Left to right: Cream-Cheese & Nut-Filled Pastry, Saffron Cheesecake, Easy Cheesecake

1. To make pastry, in a medium bowl, beat cream cheese, butter or margarine, sugar and milk until blended. In a small bowl, combine flour and baking powder. With a wooden spoon, stir flour mixture into cream-cheese mixture to make a soft dough. Knead in bowl several strokes or until smooth. Wrap with plastic wrap; refrigerate 30 minutes. Reserve egg-yolk glaze.
2. Preheat oven to 350F (175C). Grease a large baking sheet.
3. To make filling, in a medium bowl, beat butter or margarine, sugar, cream cheese and vanilla until blended. Set aside.
4. On a lightly floured surface, roll out pastry to a 16" x 10" rectangle. Spread cheese filling over pastry to within 1 inch of edges. Sprinkle nuts and raisins over cheese filling.
5. Fold 1 long pastry edge in over filling. From folded edge, roll up pastry, jelly-roll style. Brush pastry edge with egg-yolk glaze; pinch to seal. Tuck in ends of pastry. Place filled pastry, seam-side down, on greased baking sheet; brush with egg-yolk glaze.
6. Bake in preheated oven 50 to 55 minutes or until pastry is golden brown. Cool on baking sheet on a wire rack 10 minutes. Slide a long spatula under pastry; carefully remove from baking sheet. Cool completely on wire rack.
7. To serve, sift powdered sugar over roll. Cut into slices. Serve immediately or refrigerate. Makes 12 to 14 servings.

Saffron Cheesecake

Filling:
1 pinch saffron threads
1 teaspoon lemon juice
1 (8-oz.) pkg. cream cheese, room temperature
3/4 cup sugar
3 eggs, separated
2 tablespoons ground almonds
2 tablespoons grated lemon peel
3 tablespoons all-purpose flour
1/2 cup dairy sour cream
2 tablespoons butter or margarine, melted
1 cup raisins

Crust:
1 recipe Sweet Shortcrust Pastry, page 8, baked blind in
a 9-inch springform pan

To decorate:
1 tablespoon ground cinnamon

This is an old-fashioned baked cheesecake with the subtle
flavor of saffron and almonds.

1. To make filling, soak saffron in lemon juice 1 hour.
2. In a medium bowl, beat cream cheese, sugar and egg
yolks until light and fluffy.
3. Beat in almonds, lemon peel and flour until combined.
Beat in sour cream, butter or margarine, saffron with
liquid and raisins.
4. In a medium bowl, beat egg whites until stiff but not
dry. Fold in beaten egg whites. Pour filling into baked
pastry shell; smooth top.
5. Bake in preheated oven 1 hour 10 minutes or until a
wooden pick inserted off center comes out clean. Cool in
pan on a wire rack.
6. Refrigerate until served. Carefully remove side of pan.
Place on a serving plate. Sprinkle with cinnamon. Makes
10 servings.

Easy Cheesecake

Sour-Cream Filling:
2 (8-oz.) pkgs. Neufchâtel cheese, room temperature
1/2 pint dairy sour cream (1 cup)
3 eggs, separated
3/4 cup sugar
2 teaspoons grated lemon peel

Crust:
1 recipe Sweet Shortcrust Pastry, page 8, baked blind in
an 8-inch springform pan

To decorate:
Powdered sugar
Fresh strawberries or raspberries, if desired

---

1. Preheat oven to 350F (175C). To make filling, in a
medium bowl, beat cheese and sour cream until smooth.
Beat in egg yolks and sugar until thick and creamy. Stir in
lemon peel.
2. In a medium bowl, beat egg whites until stiff but not
dry. Fold beaten egg whites into cheese mixture. Pour mixture into baked pastry shell.
3. Bake in preheated oven 50 to 60 minutes or until a
wooden pick inserted off center comes out clean. Cool in
pan on a wire rack.
4. Refrigerate until served. Carefully remove side of pan.
Immediately before serving, sift powdered sugar over
cheesecake. Top with fresh fruit, if desired. Makes 8
servings.

Chocolate Cheese-Filled Gugelhupf

Filling:
1 (8-oz.) pkg. cream cheese, room temperature
2 egg yolks
1/2 cup sugar
2 tablespoons unsweetened cocoa powder
2 tablespoons dairy sour cream

Cake batter:
10 tablespoons butter or margarine, room temperature
2/3 cup sugar
3 eggs
1 cup all-purpose flour
1 teaspoon baking powder
1/4 cup milk

To decorate:
Powdered sugar

1. Preheat oven to 350F (175C). Generously grease a 9-cup gugelhupf or Bundt pan.
2. To make filling, in a medium bowl, beat cream cheese, egg yolks and sugar until blended. Beat in cocoa and sour cream until just blended. Set aside.
3. To make cake batter, in a medium bowl, beat butter or margarine and sugar until light and fluffy. Beat in eggs, 1 at a time, beating well after each addition.
4. Sift flour and baking powder into a medium bowl. Stir flour mixture into egg mixture alternately with milk, beating until blended.
5. Spoon 2/3 of cake batter into greased pan; spread evenly. Spoon chocolate-cheese filling on top of batter. Spoon remaining cake batter over chocolate-cheese filling; spread lightly.
6. Bake in preheated oven 50 to 60 minutes or until a wooden pick inserted in center comes out clean. Cool in pan on a wire rack 2 hours. Remove from pan; cool completely on wire rack.
7. Serve immediately or refrigerate. To serve, place cake on a serving plate; sift powdered sugar over cake. Makes 8 to 10 servings.

Cheese Strudel

1/4 cup butter or margarine, room temperature
1/4 cup sugar
2 egg yolks
1 (8-oz.) pkg. cream cheese, room temperature
1 (3-oz.) pkg. cream cheese, room temperature
1/2 cup whipping cream
1 teaspoon grated lemon peel
1/3 cup raisins
1/2 cup chopped walnuts
12 filo-dough sheets, thawed if frozen
1/2 cup butter or margarine, melted

To decorate:
Powdered sugar

1. Preheat oven to 375F (190C). In a medium bowl, beat butter or margarine and sugar until light and fluffy. Beat in egg yolks, 1 at a time, beating well after each addition. Beat in cream cheese until smooth. Beat in whipping cream and lemon peel until combined. Fold in raisins and walnuts.
2. Unfold filo sheets; cover with a slightly damp towel. Place a dry towel on a flat surface. Lay a filo sheet on towel; brush with melted butter or margarine. Place another filo sheet next to first sheet, overlapping edges by 2-1/2 inches; see illustration below. Brush second sheet with melted butter or margarine. Top with remaining 10 filo sheets, arranging same way, brushing each 1 with melted butter or margarine. Reserve some melted butter or margarine for finished strudel.
3. Spread filling over buttered filo sheets, leaving a 2-inch border around edge. Fold in edges. From 1 short end, carefully roll up strudel, jelly-roll style. Using towel, place filled strudel, seam-side down, on greased baking sheet. Brush with remaining melted butter or margarine.
4. Bake in preheated oven 40 minutes or until puffed and golden brown. Serve warm or at room temperature. Sift powdered sugar over strudel before serving. Makes 10 servings.

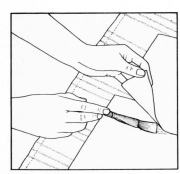
1/Brush filo sheets with butter or margarine. Overlap edges by 2-1/2 inches.

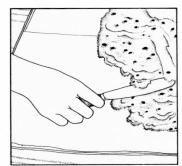
2/Spread filling over buttered filo sheets, leaving a 2-inch border around edge.

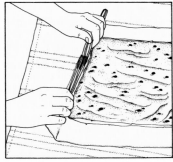
3/Fold in edges.

4/Use towel to help with rolled filled pastry.

Top to bottom: Chocolate Cheese-Filled Gugelhupf, Cheese Strudel

Sour-Cream Cheesecake

Crust:
1 (8-inch) Nut-Crumb Crust, page 8

Filling:
2 (8-oz.) pkgs. cream cheese, room temperature
1/2 cup sugar
1 teaspoon vanilla extract
3 eggs

Topping:
2 tablespoons sugar
1 teaspoon vanilla extract
1 tablespoon fresh orange juice
1 tablespoon grated lemon peel
1/2 pint dairy sour cream (1 cup)

To decorate:
Julienned orange peel

1. Preheat oven to 400F (205C). Grease an 8-inch spring-form pan. Press crust into bottom of pan.
2. To make filling, in a medium bowl, beat cream cheese, sugar and vanilla until smooth. Beat in eggs, 1 at a time, beating well after each addition. Pour filling over crust in pan; smooth top.
3. Bake 20 minutes. While cheesecake is baking, make topping.
4. To make topping, in a medium bowl, combine all topping ingredients. Pour over partially-baked cheesecake in pan; smooth top. Bake 20 minutes more or until topping is set. Cool in pan on a wire rack.
5. Refrigerate until served. To serve, carefully remove side of pan; place cake on a serving plate. Decorate with orange peel. Makes 8 servings.

Blueberry & Lemon Cheesecake

1 recipe Sweet Shortcrust Pastry, page 8

Filling:
1 (8-oz.) pkg. cream cheese, room temperature
1 tablespoon dairy sour cream
2 tablespoons lemon juice
1 tablespoon grated lemon peel
2/3 cup powdered sugar, sifted
3 eggs, beaten

Topping:
2 cups fresh or frozen thawed blueberries
1/4 cup sugar
1 tablespoon cornstarch
Pinch of salt
2 tablespoons lemon juice
1/4 cup water

1. Grease a 9-inch springform pan. Prepare pastry as directed on page 8. Press pastry into bottom of greased pan. Bake blind as directed on page 8. Cool on a wire rack.
2. Preheat oven to 350F (175C). To make filling, in a medium bowl, beat cheese, sour cream, lemon juice and lemon peel until blended. Beat in powdered sugar and eggs until light and creamy. Pour filling over baked pastry in pan.
3. Bake in preheated oven 40 minutes or until a wooden pick inserted off center comes out clean. Cool in pan on a wire rack while making topping.
4. Meanwhile, make topping. To make topping, in a medium saucepan, combine blueberries, sugar, cornstarch and salt. Stir in lemon juice and water.
5. Simmer mixture about 3 minutes or until thickened, stirring constantly. Let cool 10 minutes.
6. Pour topping over cooled cheesecake; smooth top. Refrigerate at least 4 hours or until served.
7. To serve, carefully remove side of pan; place cake on a serving plate. Makes 6 servings.

Left to right: Sour-Cream Cheesecake, Blueberry & Lemon Cheesecake, Pecan Cheesecake

Pecan-Topped Cheesecake

Filling:
2 (8-oz.) pkgs. cream cheese, room temperature
1 (3-oz.) pkg. cream cheese, room temperature
1 cup sugar
Pinch of salt
1 tablespoon vanilla sugar or 1 tablespoon sugar and 1
    teaspoon vanilla extract
1 teaspoon grated lemon peel
4 eggs, separated
1/2 cup all-purpose flour, sifted
1/2 cup whipping cream

Crust:
1 (8-inch) Nut-Crumb Crust, page 8

To decorate:
Whipped cream
Pecan halves

1. Preheat oven to 325F (165C). To make filling, in a medium bowl, beat cream cheese, 1/2 cup sugar, salt, vanilla sugar or 1 tablespoon sugar and vanilla and lemon peel. Beat in egg yolks, 1 at a time, beating well after each addition. Beat in flour.
2. In a small bowl, beat cream until soft peaks form. Fold whipped cream into cream-cheese mixture. In a medium bowl, beat egg whites until stiff but not dry. Beat in remaining 1/2 cup sugar, 1 tablespoon at a time. Beat until stiff and glossy. Fold egg-white mixture into cream-cheese mixture.
3. Grease an 8-inch springform pan. Press crust into bottom of greased pan. Pour mixture into crust-lined pan; smooth top.
4. Bake in preheated oven 1 hour 15 minutes or until a wooden pick inserted off center comes out clean. Cool in pan on a wire rack. Refrigerate 3 to 4 hours or until served.
5. Carefully remove side of pan; place cheesecake on a serving plate. Spoon whipped cream into a pastry bag fitted with a large star tip. Pipe a swirl of whipped cream around top of cheesecake; arrange pecan halves on cream. Makes 10 servings.

Cheese Ring & Fruit Diplomat

Double recipe Orange Sauce, page 14
1 (1/4-oz.) envelope plus 1 teaspoon unflavored gelatin
1/4 cup water
1-1/2 cups ricotta cheese, drained
2/3 cup sugar
3 eggs, separated
1 tablespoon grated orange peel
1 teaspoon grated lemon peel
2 tablespoons lemon juice
2/3 cup dairy sour cream
3/4 cup whipping cream
1/4 cup apricot jam
2 tablespoons water
1-1/2 lb. fresh fruit
1 baked 11-inch Genoise Sponge layer, page 11

Use any combination of fresh fruit in season, such as cherries, kiwifruit, oranges, apples, peaches, pears, apricots, raspberries or strawberries to make this special dessert. Choose fruits that compliment each other in color, texture and flavor.

1. Prepare orange sauce as directed on page 14; cover and refrigerate.
2. In a small saucepan, combine gelatin and 1/4 cup water. Stir well; let stand 3 minutes. Stir over low heat until gelatin dissolves; cool to room temperature.
3. In a medium bowl, beat ricotta cheese, sugar and egg yolks until blended. Beat in orange peel, lemon peel, lemon juice and sour cream. Gradually beat in cooled gelatin mixture. Refrigerate 20 to 30 minutes or until mixture mounds when dropped from a spoon.
4. Brush a 6-1/2-cup ring mold with vegetable oil; set aside. In a medium bowl, beat whipping cream until soft peaks form. Fold whipped cream into ricotta-cheese mixture. In a medium bowl, beat egg whites until stiff but not dry; fold into cheese mixture. Pour into oiled mold; smooth top. Refrigerate several hours or until firm.
5. To assemble, press apricot jam through a sieve into a small saucepan. Stir in 2 tablespoons water. Cook over low heat, stirring, until jam melts. Cool slightly.
6. Place sponge cake on a large serving plate; brush with melted jam. Run a knife around edge of mold to loosen. Invert cheese ring onto sponge cake. Rinse a towel under hot running water; wring dry. Wrap hot towel around outside of mold. Let stand 10 to 15 seconds. Carefully remove mold. Arrange some fruit around edge of ring. Fill center of ring with remaining fruit. Refrigerate until served. Serve with Orange Sauce. Makes 14 to 16 servings.

Heavenly Cake

1 recipe Cinnamon Pastry, from Chocolate-Cinnamon Torte, page 44
2 tablespoons sliced almonds
1 recipe Cheese-Cream Filling, from Strawberry & Cream-Cheese Shortcake, page 47
1 cup red-currant jelly (about 8 oz.)

To decorate:
Fresh raspberries or other fresh fruit

This is a summer version of Chocolate-Cinnamon Torte, page 44. This version is much lighter and less rich. For best flavor, refrigerate two days before serving.

1. Roll out and bake pastry circles as directed on page 44, scattering almonds over 1 circle before baking. Cool on wire racks.
2. Prepare filling as directed on page 47. Set almond-coated circle aside. Spread 1/3 of jelly over each remaining pastry circle. Spread each jelly-coated circle with 1/3 of filling.
3. Place 1 filling-covered circle on a serving plate. Top with remaining filling-covered circles. Place almond-topped pastry circle on top. Refrigerate until served. Top with fresh fruit immediately before serving. Makes 4 servings.

Clockwise from left: Cheese Ring & Fruit Diplomat; Orange Sauce, page 14; Heavenly Cake

Strawberry Cheesecake

1 (8-inch) Shortcrust Pastry, page 8

Filling:
2 cups fresh or thawed frozen strawberries
3 tablespoons kirsch
2/3 cup sugar
2 (1/4-oz.) envelopes unflavored gelatin (2 tablespoons)
5 tablespoons water
2 (8-oz.) pkgs. cream cheese, room temperature
3 eggs, separated
1/2 cup dairy sour cream

To decorate:
1-1/2 cups whipped cream
Toast almond slices

---

1. Lightly grease bottom of an 8-inch springform pan. Prepare pastry dough as directed on page 8. Press dough into bottom of springform pan. Bake blind as directed on page 8. Cool in pan on a wire rack. Remove from pan. Clean and grease pan. Line side of pan with waxed paper. Place baked pastry in pan.
2. Reserve 4 strawberries for decoration. In a medium bowl, combine remaining strawberries, kirsch and sugar; let stand 1 to 2 hours. In a blender or food processor with a steel blade, process strawberries and their juices until smooth.
3. In a small saucepan, combine gelatin and water. Stir well; let stand 3 minutes. Stir over low heat until gelatin dissolves; cool to room temperature. In a medium bowl, combine cream cheese and pureed strawberries. Beat until combined.
4. Beat in egg yolks, 1 at a time, beating well after each addition. Beat in sour cream and cooled gelatin. Refrigerate until mixture mounds when dropped from a spoon.
5. In a medium bowl, beat egg whites until stiff but not dry; fold beaten egg whites into filling. Pour mixture into pastry-lined pan; refrigerate 5 to 6 hours or until set.
6. To serve, carefully remove side of pan and waxed paper. Set cake on a serving plate. Spread 3/4 cup whipped cream over top. Spoon remaining whipped cream into a pastry bag fitted with a star or rosette tip. Pipe rosettes around edge of cheesecake. Arrange reserved strawberries and toasted almond slices in center. Makes 8 servings.

Variation
Raspberry Cheesecake: Substitute raspberries for strawberries. Substitute a raspberry brandy for kirsch.

Wild-Blueberry Cheesecake

1 baked 10-inch Sponge Layer, page 10
1 (15-oz.) can wild blueberries
3 tablespoons Cointreau

Filling:
1 (1/4-oz.) envelope unflavored gelatin (1 tablespoon)
5 tablespoons orange juice
4 (3-oz.) pkgs. cream cheese, room temperature
1/2 cup sugar
3 eggs, separated
1 tablespoon grated orange peel
1/2 pint whipping cream (1 cup)

To decorate:
Chopped pistachios
Sweetened whipped cream
Julienned orange peel

---

1. Grease bottom and side of a 10-inch springform pan. Cut sponge layer in half horizontally. Place 1/2 of sponge layer, cut-side up, in bottom of lined pan. Reserve remaining half for another use.
2. Drain blueberries, reserving 6 tablespoons juice. Combine Cointreau with reserved blueberry juice; sprinkle over sponge layer. Set aside 1/3 cup blueberries. Scatter remaining blueberries over sponge layer. Set aside.
3. To make filling, in a small saucepan, combine gelatin and orange juice. Stir well; let stand 3 minutes. Stir over low heat until gelatin dissolves; cool to room temperature.
4. In a large bowl, beat cream cheese and sugar until light and fluffy. Beat in egg yolks, 1 at a time, beating well after each addition. Beat in orange peel and cooled gelatin until blended. Refrigerate mixture about 20 minutes or until mixture mounds when dropped from a spoon.
5. In a medium bowl, beat cream until soft peaks form. Fold whipped cream into cream-cheese mixture. In a medium bowl, beat egg whites until stiff but not dry. Fold beaten egg whites into cheese mixture.
6. Pour cheese mixture into cake-lined pan; smooth top. Refrigerate 3 to 4 hours or until served.
7. To serve, run a knife around inside edge of pan. Carefully remove side of pan; place cheesecake on a serving plate. Decorate center with reserved blueberries and chopped pistachios. Spoon whipped cream into a pastry bag fitted with a star or rosette tip. Pipe whipped cream around blueberries; decorate with orange peel. Makes 10 to 12 servings.

Clockwise from left: Wild-Blueberry Cheesecake, Summer Meringue Cheesecake, Strawberry Cheesecake

Summer Meringue Cheesecake

Meringue:
4 egg whites
1 cup sugar

Filling:
1 recipe Cheese-Cream Filling, from Strawberry &
Cream-Cheese Shortcake, page 47
3 cups fresh or thawed frozen raspberries

1. Preheat oven to 275F (135C). Line 2 baking sheets with parchment paper. Draw 2 (9-1/2-inch) circles on parchment paper.
2. To make meringue, in a medium bowl, beat egg whites until soft peaks form. Gradually beat in sugar; beat until stiff and glossy.
3. Spoon 1/2 of meringue mixture into each circle; smooth top lightly.
4. Bake in preheated oven about 1-1/2 hours or until meringues are dry and crisp. Cool on wire racks.
5. Prepare filling as directed on page 47. Place 1 meringue layer on a serving plate; spread with 1/2 of filling. Reserve a few raspberries for decoration; arrange remaining raspberries evenly over filling. Spread remaining filling over raspberries; top with remaining meringue layer.
6. Arrange reserved raspberries in center of cake; serve immediately. Makes 8 servings.

Chocolate-Cinnamon Torte

Cinnamon Pastry:
5 teaspoons ground cinnamon
1-1/4 cups sugar
10 tablespoons butter or margarine, room temperature
4 egg yolks
2 cups all-purpose flour
1/4 teaspoon baking powder

Filling:
2-1/4 cups whipping cream
10 oz. semisweet chocolate, chopped
2 (3-oz.) pkgs. cream cheese, room temperature
2 tablespoons granulated sugar
2 tablespoons dark rum
1 teaspoon vanilla extract
2 to 3 tablespoons powdered sugar

To decorate:
Chocolate coffee-bean candies
Sliced toasted almonds

1. Preheat oven to 350F (175C). Remove sides and grease bottoms only of 2 (9-inch) springform pans. To make pastry, in a small bowl, combine 2 teaspoons cinnamon with 1/2 cup sugar; set aside. In a medium bowl, beat butter or margarine and remaining 3/4 cup sugar until light and fluffy. Beat in egg yolks until thoroughly blended.
2. Sift flour, remaining 3 teaspoons cinnamon and baking powder over egg mixture; stir in with a wooden spoon to make a soft dough. Knead dough in bowl several strokes or until smooth.
3. Divide pastry into 4 equal pieces. On a lightly floured surface, roll or pat out 2 pieces of pastry into 9-inch circles. Use pastry to line bottoms of pans. Sprinkle each pastry circle with 2 tablespoons reserved cinnamon-sugar mixture.
4. Bake in preheated oven 15 to 18 minutes or until just firm. Remove from pan bottoms; cool completely on wire racks. Repeat with remaining 2 pieces of pastry and remaining cinnamon-sugar mixture. Score 1 baked pastry round into 10 to 12 equal wedges while still warm; do not cut completely through.
5. To make filling, pour 3/4 cup whipping cream into a medium saucepan. Cook over medium heat until tiny bubbles form around edge of pan. Remove from heat. Gradually add chocolate; stir until chocolate melts and mixture is smooth. Pour into a large bowl; cool to room temperature.
6. With an electric mixer, beat chocolate mixture until doubled in volume. Beat in cream cheese, granulated sugar and rum until blended. Spoon 3/4 cup chocolate-cream mixture into a pastry bag fitted with a star tip. Spread remaining chocolate-cream mixture over 3 unscored pastry rounds.
7. In a medium bowl, beat remaining 1-1/2 cups cream until soft peaks form. Beat in vanilla and powdered sugar. Spoon about 3/4 cup whipped cream into a pastry bag fitted with a star tip. Spread remaining whipped cream over chocolate-cream-covered pastry rounds. Place 1 cream-topped layer on a serving plate; top with remaining 2 cream-topped layers, cream-side up.

8. Place scored pastry round on top of filled layers. Pipe alternating rosettes of reserved chocolate cream and plain whipped cream in center of each scored wedge. Decorate with coffee-bean candies and sliced almonds. Refrigerate until served. Makes 10 to 12 servings.

Chocolate-Hazelnut Cheesecake

1 (10-inch) Hazelnut-Crumb Crust, page 7
20 dark chocolate thins

Filling:
3 oz. semisweet chocolate, chopped
2 tablespoons hot water
1 (1/4-oz.) envelope plus 1 teaspoon unflavored gelatin
1/4 cup milk
2 (8-oz.) pkgs. cream cheese, room temperature
3/4 cup sugar
4 eggs, separated
1/4 cup dark rum
1/2 pint whipping cream (1 cup)
1/3 cup finely chopped toasted hazelnuts

To decorate:
Sweetened whipped cream
Whole hazelnuts

1. Grease a 10-inch springform pan. Prepare crust as directed on page 7; press onto bottom of greased pan. Arrange chocolate thins around inside edge of pan, pressing chocolate lightly into crust for support. Refrigerate while preparing filling.
2. To make filling, in a small saucepan over low heat, combine chocolate and water; stir until smooth. Cool to room temperature.
3. In another small saucepan, combine gelatin and milk. Stir well; let stand 3 minutes. Stir over low heat until gelatin dissolves; cool to room temperature.
4. In a large bowl, beat cream cheese and sugar until light and fluffy. Beat in egg yolks, melted chocolate and rum until blended. Gradually beat in cooled gelatin until blended. Beat in cream until blended. Refrigerate about 30 minutes or until mixture mounds when dropped from a spoon.
5. In a medium bowl, beat egg whites until stiff but not dry. Fold in beaten egg whites. Fold in chopped hazelnuts.
6. Pour mixture into chocolate-lined pan; smooth top. Refrigerate 5 to 6 hours or until served.
7. To serve, remove side of pan; place cheesecake on a serving plate. Spoon whipped cream into a pastry bag fitted with a star tip. Pipe whipped cream in stars on top of cheesecake; decorate with whole hazelnuts. Makes 12 to 14 servings.

Raspberry-Hazelnut Torte

2 cups all-purpose flour
2/3 cup sugar
1 cup finely ground hazelnuts
1 cup butter or margarine
1 recipe Cream-Cheese Filling, from Strawberry &
　Cream-Cheese Shortcake, page 47
2 tablespoons raspberry brandy
2 cups fresh or thawed frozen raspberries

To decorate:
About 2 cups sweetened whipped cream

1. Preheat oven to 325F (165C). Grease and flour a large baking sheet.
2. In a medium bowl, combine flour, sugar and hazelnuts until blended. With a pastry blender or 2 knives, cut in butter or margarine until mixture resembles coarse crumbs. Shape into a flattened ball.
3. Divide pastry into 2 equal pieces. On a lightly floured surface, roll out each piece of pastry to an 8-inch circle. Place circles on prepared baking sheet.
4. Bake in preheated oven 20 to 25 minutes or until golden brown. Cool on baking sheet on a wire rack 10 minutes. Cut 1 pastry round into 8 equal wedges while still warm. Remove from baking sheet; cool completely on wire rack.
5. Prepare filling as directed on page 47, substituting raspberry brandy for Grand Marnier.
6. To assemble, place whole pastry round on a serving plate; spread with filling. Arrange pastry wedges in a circle on top of filling, pressing 1 edge slightly into filling; see photo. Place a raspberry between each wedge for support. Fill center with raspberries. Spoon whipped cream into a pastry bag fitted with a large star tip. Fill space under each wedge with piped whipped cream. Serve immediately. Makes 8 servings.

Clockwise from left: Chocolate-Hazelnut Cheesecake, Raspberry-Hazelnut Torte, Chocolate-Cinnamon Torte

Lindy's Style Cheesecake

Pastry:
1-1/2 cups sifted all-purpose flour
1/4 cup sugar
1 teaspoon grated lemon peel
1/2 cup butter or margarine, room temperature
2 egg yolks, beaten
1 egg white, beaten

Filling:
4 (8-oz.) pkgs. cream cheese, room temperature
1-1/2 cups sugar
3 tablespoons all-purpose flour
2 tablespoons grated orange peel
1 tablespoon grated lemon peel
2 egg yolks
5 eggs
1/2 cup whipping cream

To decorate:
Powdered sugar
Candied orange peel

---

1. To make pastry, in a medium bowl, combine flour, sugar and lemon peel. Work butter or margarine and egg yolks into flour mixture with your fingertips to make a smooth dough. Wrap dough in plastic wrap; refrigerate 30 minutes.

2. Preheat oven to 400F (205C). Grease a 10-inch spring-form pan. On a lightly floured surface, roll out 1/2 of pastry to a 10-inch circle; use pastry to line bottom of greased pan. Prick pastry with a fork.

3. Bake in preheated oven 15 minutes or until golden. Cool in pan on a wire rack. Press remaining pastry around inside edge of pan, pressing pastry about 1-1/2 inches up side of pan and joining pastry firmly to bottom crust. Brush bottom and side of pastry with beaten egg white to seal. Increase oven temperature to 450F (230C).

4. To make filling, in a large bowl, beat cream cheese, sugar and flour until light and fluffy. Beat in orange peel, lemon peel and egg yolks until blended. Add eggs, 1 at a time, beating well after each addition. Stir in cream. Pour cheese mixture into pastry-lined pan; smooth top.

5. Bake in preheated oven 15 minutes. Reduce oven temperature to 225F (105C). Bake 1-1/2 hours or until center is set. Turn oven off; leave cheesecake in oven 1 hour. Cool completely in pan on a wire rack. Refrigerate until served.

6. To serve, carefully remove side of pan; place cheesecake on a serving plate. Sift powdered sugar over top; decorate with candied orange peel. Makes 12 to 14 servings.

Left to right: Lindy's Style Cheesecake with Apricot Sauce, Strawberry & Cream-Cheese Shortcake

Apricot Sauce

2 cups apricot jam
1/4 cup sugar
1 cup water
1 tablespoon cornstarch
2 tablespoons water
3 tablespoons lemon juice or kirsch

---

1. In a small pan over medium heat, combine jam, sugar and 1 cup water. Stir until sugar dissolves. Boil 5 minutes, stirring occasionally.

2. Press jam mixture through a sieve into a clean small saucepan. In a small bowl, blend cornstarch with 2 tablespoons water. Stir cornstarch mixture into sieved jam mixture. Cook over low heat, stirring, until thickened.

3. Cool slightly; stir in lemon juice. Refrigerate until chilled.

4. Serve with chilled Lindy's Style Cheesecake or other cheesecake. Makes about 3 cups.

Strawberry & Cream-Cheese Shortcake

1 recipe Sour-Cream Pastry, from Apricot Cheesecake,
  page 16
2 cups fresh or thawed strawberries
1 tablespoon sugar

Cream-Cheese Filling:
1 (8-oz.) pkg. cream cheese, room temperature
1/3 cup sugar
2 tablespoons dairy sour cream
2 tablespoons Grand Marnier
1/2 cup whipping cream

To decorate:
1 cup whipped cream

---

*This is an interesting variation of traditional strawberry
shortcake.*

1. Preheat oven to 375F (190C). Prepare pastry as directed
on page 16. Divide pastry in half. On a lightly floured
surface, roll out each piece into an 8-inch circle. Place circles on ungreased baking sheets.
2. Bake in preheated oven 20 minutes or until golden
brown. Cool pastry on baking sheets on wire racks 10 minutes. Remove from baking sheets; cool completely on wire
racks.
3. Reserve 5 strawberries for decoration. Slice enough
strawberries to make 1/2 cup. Crush remaining strawberries in a medium bowl; stir in sliced strawberries and
sugar.
4. To make filling, beat cream cheese and sugar until light
and fluffy. Beat in sour cream and Grand Marnier. In a
small bowl, beat whipping cream until soft peaks form.
Fold whipped cream into cream-cheese mixture.
5. Place 1 cooled pastry round on a serving plate; spread
with 1/2 of cream-cheese filling. Spread strawberry mixture over filling. Cover strawberries with remaining
filling. Top with remaining pastry. Refrigerate until
chilled.
6. To serve, spread whipped cream on top of cake; decorate with reserved strawberries. Makes 6 servings.

Lemon-Curd & Cheese Torte

1 baked 10-inch Genoise Sponge, page 11
3 tablespoons water
1/3 cup sugar
3 tablespoons dark rum

Filling:
2/3 cup raisins or currants
2 tablespoons dark rum
2 (1/4-oz.) envelopes unflavored gelatin (2 tablespoons)
1/3 cup milk
1-1/2 cups small-curd cottage cheese, drained
1/2 cup sugar
1 cup lemon curd, page 26
1-1/2 cups whipping cream
2 tablespoons chopped pistachios

To decorate:
Powdered sugar
Sweetened whipped cream
Toasted sliced almonds

1. Grease a 10-inch springform pan. Cut cake in half horizontally. Place 1 half, cut-side up, in bottom of greased pan. Cut remaining layer into 10 equal wedges; set aside.
2. In a small saucepan over medium heat, cook water and sugar, stirring, until sugar dissolves and mixture comes to a boil. Boil 1 minute. Let cool slightly. Stir in 3 tablespoons rum. Sprinkle rum syrup over cake in pan; set aside.
3. To make filling, in a small bowl, combine raisins or currants and rum. Set aside.
4. In a small saucepan, combine gelatin and milk. Stir well; let stand 3 minutes. Stir over low heat until gelatin dissolves; cool to room temperature.
5. In a medium bowl, beat cottage cheese until smooth. Beat in sugar and lemon curd until blended. Beat in cooled gelatin. Refrigerate 20 to 30 minutes or until mixture mounds when dropped from a spoon.
6. In a medium bowl, beat cream until soft peaks form. Fold whipped cream into cottage-cheese mixture. Fold in pistachios and raisins or currants with rum.
7. Pour mixture over cake in pan; smooth top. Arrange reserved cake wedges on top of filling. Refrigerate 4 to 5 hours or until served.
8. To serve, run a knife around inside edge of pan. Remove side of pan; place torte on a serving plate. Sift powdered sugar over torte. Spoon whipped cream into a pastry bag fitted with a rosette tip. Pipe whipped cream in center of each cake wedge; decorate with sliced almonds. Makes 10 servings.

Rose Cheesecake

1 recipe Sour-Cream Pastry, from Apricot Cheesecake, page 16

Filling:
1/2 cup butter or margarine, room temperature
2-1/2 (8-oz.) pkgs. cream cheese, room temperature
1 cup plus 2 tablespoons sugar
4 eggs, separated
1/4 cup chopped candied orange peel
1 teaspoon grated lemon peel
1 teaspoon rose water
1-1/2 tablespoons ground almonds
1/2 cup rose-petal jam or seedless red-raspberry jam

To decorate:
Powdered sugar
Fresh roses, if desired

Rose water, orange-blossom water and a rose jam made from crushed rose petals have been used in Middle Eastern cooking for centuries. The jam is also used in Poland. Rose-petal jam can be bought in Middle Eastern and Greek food stores.

1. Preheat oven to 400F (205C). Prepare pastry as directed on page 16. On a lightly floured surface, roll out pastry to an 11-inch circle. Use pastry to line an 8-inch springform pan, pressing pastry 1 inch up side. Prick pastry with a fork. Line with foil; fill with pie weights or dried beans.
2. Bake in preheated oven 10 minutes. Remove foil and pie weights or beans. Reduce oven temperature to 375F (190C). Bake 5 to 7 minutes more or until pastry is golden brown. Cool in pan on a wire rack before filling.
3. To make filling, beat butter or margarine, cream cheese and sugar until light and fluffy. Beat in egg yolks, 1 at a time, beating well after each addition. Stir in candied peel, lemon peel and rose water.
4. In a medium bowl, beat egg whites until stiff but not dry; fold beaten egg whites and ground almonds into cream-cheese mixture.
5. Spread jam over bottom of cooled pastry. Pour in filling; smooth top.
6. Bake in preheated oven 1 hour or until a wooden pick inserted off center comes out clean. Cool in pan on a wire rack. Refrigerate until served.
7. To serve, carefully remove side of pan; place cake on a serving plate. Immediately before serving, sift powdered sugar over cake; decorate with roses, if desired. Makes 8 servings.

Clockwise from left: Lemon-Curd & Cheese Torte, Rose Cheesecake, Chocolate & Ginger Cheesecake

Chocolate & Ginger Cheesecake

1 (8-inch) Crumb Crust, page 7, made with gingersnaps

Filling:
4 oz. semisweet chocolate, chopped
2 teaspoons unflavored gelatin powder
3 tablespoons water
1 (8-oz) pkg. cream cheese, room temperature
1/2 cup plus 2 tablespoons firmly packed light-brown sugar
1 teaspoon ground ginger
Pinch of salt
2 eggs, separated
1/2 pint whipping cream (1 cup)
1/4 cup ginger marmalade

To decorate:
Crystallized ginger

This cheesecake is richly flavored with chocolate and ginger.

1. Grease bottom and side of an 8-inch springform pan. Prepare crust as directed on page 7, using gingersnap crumbs. Press crust into bottom of greased pan. In a small heavy saucepan over very low heat, melt chocolate; stir until smooth. Cool to room temperature.
2. In a small saucepan, combine gelatin and water. Stir well; let stand 3 minutes. Stir over low heat until gelatin dissolves; cool to room temperature.
3. In a medium bowl, beat cream cheese, 1/2 cup brown sugar, ginger, cooled chocolate and salt. Beat in egg yolks, 1 at a time, beating well after each addition. Beat in cooled gelatin. Refrigerate 20 to 30 minutes or until mixture mounds when dropped from a spoon.
4. In a medium bowl, beat cream until soft peaks form. Spoon 1/2 cup whipped cream into a pastry bag fitted with a rosette tip. Fold remaining cream into cream-cheese mixture.
5. In a medium bowl, beat egg whites until soft peaks form. Gradually beat in remaining 2 tablespoons brown sugar; beat until stiff and glossy. Fold into cream-cheese mixture.
6. Spread marmalade over crumb crust. Pour in filling; smooth top. Refrigerate 3 to 4 hours or until set.
7. To serve, run a knife around edge of cheesecake. Carefully remove side of pan; place cheesecake on a serving plate. Decorate with reserved whipped cream and crystallized ginger. Makes 8 servings.

Clockwise from left: Lemon Japonais, Toasted Almond Torte,
Cream-Cheese Mille Feuilles

Lemon Japonais

Meringue:
2 egg whites
1/2 cup sugar
1/2 cup ground toasted hazelnuts
1 tablespoon all-purpose flour
3 oz. semisweet chocolate, chopped

Filling:
6 tablespoons lemon curd, page 26
1 recipe filling, from Lemon Cheesecake, page 25
3 tablespoons apricot jam
2 tablespoons water
1 baked 9-inch Sponge Layer, page 10
1/2 cup chopped toasted hazelnuts

To decorate:
Chocolate curls
Lemon slices

1. Preheat oven to 300F (150C). Grease bottom and side of a 9-inch springform pan. Line bottom with waxed paper.
2. In a medium bowl, beat egg whites until soft peaks form. Gradually beat in sugar until stiff and glossy. Fold in flour and ground hazelnuts. Spoon mixture into prepared pan; smooth top.
3. Bake in preheated oven 1 hour. Cool in pan on a wire rack 10 minutes. Carefully remove from pan; peel off waxed paper. Cool on a wire rack.
4. Melt chocolate in a small heavy saucepan over very low heat. Cool slightly. Spoon cooled chocolate over cooled meringue. Let stand until chocolate is set.
5. Wash and dry springform pan. Line clean pan with waxed paper; lightly oil sides. Place meringue in pan, chocolate-side down. Spread lemon curd on top of meringue.
6. Prepare filling as directed on page 25; set aside. In a small saucepan over low heat, stir apricot jam and water until jam melts. Press through a sieve into a small bowl. Brush a thin layer of jam over sponge cake; reserve remaining jam. Place sponge cake, apricot-glazed side up, over lemon curd in pan.
7. Pour filling over cake in pan; smooth top. Refrigerate 3 to 4 hours or until set.
8. To serve, carefully remove side of pan; remove waxed paper. Place cake on a serving plate. Brush sides of sponge cake and meringue with remaining apricot glaze; press chopped hazelnuts against glazed side. Decorate top with chocolate curls and lemon slices. Makes 10 to 12 servings.

Toasted Almond Torte

1 recipe Sweet Shortcrust Pastry, page 8

Choux Paste:
1/4 cup butter or margarine
1/2 cup water
2 teaspoons sugar
1/2 cup all-purpose flour
2 eggs
1/2 cup sliced almonds

Filling:
1 (1/4-oz.) envelope unflavored gelatin (1 tablespoon)
1/4 cup milk
1 (8-oz.) pkg. cream cheese, room temperature
1/3 cup sugar
3 egg yolks
1 teaspoon grated lemon peel
1/2 pint whipping cream (1 cup)
3 tablespoons apricot jam, melted, cooled
3 tablespoons strawberry or raspberry jam

To decorate:
Nectarine or peach slices
Powdered sugar

1. Make pastry as directed on page 8. Preheat oven to 400F (205C). Grease bottom of a 10-1/2- or 11-inch fluted tart pan or flan pan with a removable bottom. Pat pastry onto bottom of greased pan, pressing pastry well into fluted edges. Prick with a fork.
2. Bake in preheated oven 10 minutes. Reduce oven temperature to 375F (190C). Bake 5 to 7 minutes or until golden. Cool 15 minutes in pan on a wire rack. Remove from pan; cool completely on wire rack. Increase oven temperature to 450F (230C).
3. Line 2 baking sheets with parchment paper. Draw 3 (8- or 9-inch) circles on parchment-lined baking sheets. To make choux paste, in a medium saucepan over medium heat, combine butter or margarine, water and sugar. Bring to a boil. Add flour all at once. Stir with a wooden spoon until dough forms a ball and comes away from side of pan. Let cool slightly. Beat in eggs, 1 at a time, beating well after each addition.
4. Spread choux paste inside each circle on lined baking sheets, filling circles. Sprinkle with sliced almonds.
5. Bake in preheated oven 10 to 12 minutes or until puffed and golden brown. Reverse position of baking sheets after 5 minutes. Remove from baking sheets; peel off lining paper. Cool completely on wire racks.
6. To make filling, in a small saucepan, combine gelatin and milk. Stir well; let stand 3 minutes. Stir over low heat until gelatin dissolves; cool to room temperature. In a medium bowl, beat cream cheese and sugar until light and fluffy. Beat in egg yolks and lemon peel until blended. Gradually beat in cooled gelatin until blended.
7. In a medium bowl, beat whipping cream until soft peaks form. Fold whipped cream into cream-cheese mixture. Refrigerate until mixture mounds when dropped from spoon.
8. To assemble torte, place pastry on a large serving plate; brush with apricot jam. Place 1 choux layer, almond-side up, in center of pastry; spread with 1/2 of cheese filling. Spread strawberry jam over second choux layer; place layer, jam-side up, on cheese filling. Spread remaining cheese filling over jam-covered layer. Top with remaining choux layer, almond-side up. Refrigerate until served.
9. To decorate, arrange nectarine or peach slices around bottom of pastry base. Sift powdered sugar over top. Makes 10 to 12 servings.

Cream-Cheese Mille Feuilles

1 (17-1/2 oz.) pkg. frozen puff pastry, thawed

Filling:
1-1/2 cups sifted powdered sugar
1 (1/4-oz.) envelope unflavored gelatin (1 tablespoon)
6 egg yolks
1 cup milk
1 teaspoon vanilla extract
2 (8-oz.) pkgs. cream cheese, room temperature
1/2 pint whipping cream (1 cup)
1/3 cup chopped candied lemon peel
1/4 cup apricot jam, melted, cooled

To decorate:
Powdered sugar

1. Preheat oven to 425F (220C). On a lightly floured surface, unfold 1 pastry sheet; lay flat. Cover and refrigerate remaining pastry sheet. Cut pastry into a 10-inch circle. Remove side of a 10-inch springform pan. Place pastry circle on pan bottom; prick with a fork.
2. Bake in preheated oven 15 to 20 minutes or until golden brown and puffed. Remove from pan bottom; cool completely on a wire rack.
3. Repeat steps 1 and 2 with remaining sheet of pastry, cutting baked pastry circle into 10 equal triangles while still warm. Cool on a wire rack.
4. To make filling, in a medium saucepan, combine powdered sugar and gelatin until blended. Stir in egg yolks; gradually stir in milk until smooth. Let stand 3 minutes. Cook over low heat, stirring constantly, until mixture thickens. Do not boil. Cool slightly. Stir in vanilla. Pour custard into a large bowl; cover surface of custard with a sheet of waxed paper to prevent a skin from forming. Refrigerate until chilled.
5. In a large bowl, beat cream cheese until fluffy. Gradually beat in chilled custard. In a medium bowl, beat cream until soft peaks form. Fold whipped cream into cream-cheese mixture. Fold in candied lemon peel.
6. Lightly grease bottom of a 10-inch springform pan. Place cooled pastry circle in bottom of greased pan; brush with melted apricot jam. Pour cream-cheese mixture over pastry circle in pan; smooth top. Arrange pastry triangles in a circle on top of cream-cheese mixture, pressing 1 edge into filling. Refrigerate 4 to 5 hours or until served.
7. To serve, run a knife around inside edge of pan. Carefully remove side of pan; place cheesecake on a serving plate. Sift powdered sugar over cheesecake immediately before serving. Makes 10 servings.

Exotic Cheesecakes

Mocha & Chestnut Cheesecake Roll

1 recipe Chocolate Sponge Layer, page 10
2 tablespoons sugar

Filling:
2 teaspoons instant coffee powder
1 teaspoon boiling water
1 (8-oz.) pkg. cream cheese, room temperature
1/4 cup sugar
2 tablespoons coffee-flavored liqueur
1/3 (15-1/2-oz.) can unsweetened chestnut puree
1/2 cup whipping cream

To decorate:
Chocolate Rounds, opposite

1. Preheat oven to 350F (175C). Line a 13" x 9" baking pan with waxed paper, leaving a 2-inch overlap all around. Grease paper.
2. Prepare sponge-layer batter as directed on page 10. Pour batter into prepared pan; smooth top.
3. Bake in preheated oven 25 to 30 minutes or until center springs back when lightly pressed.
4. Place a clean towel on a flat surface; sprinkle with sugar. Invert cake onto sugared towel. Remove pan. Carefully peel off paper. Trim edges of cake. Starting from 1 short end, roll up cake and towel. Cool rolled cake completely on a wire rack.
5. To make filling, in a small bowl, dissolve coffee in boiling water; cool to room temperature. In a medium bowl, beat cream cheese, sugar, cooled coffee and liqueur until light and fluffy. Beat in chestnut puree. In a medium bowl, beat whipping cream until soft peaks form; fold into cheese mixture.
6. Unroll cake. Spread 2/3 of filling to within 1/2 inch of edges. Reroll filled cake, without towel; place, seam-side down, on a serving plate.
7. Spoon remaining filling into a pastry bag fitted with a large star tip; pipe filling in center of roll. Decorate with Chocolate Rounds. Refrigerate until served. Makes 6 servings.

Cheesecake Alaska

1 recipe Pistachio Filling, from Pistachio Diplomat, page 57
1 recipe Sweet Shortcrust Pastry, page 8
3 egg whites
3/4 cup sugar
2 tablespoons chopped pistachio nuts

1. Line a 9" x 5" loaf pan with waxed paper, extending paper 1 inch above sides. Prepare Pistachio Filling as directed on page 57. Pour filling into lined pan. Freeze until firm.
2. Preheat oven to 400F (205C). Prepare pastry as directed on page 8. On a lightly floured surface, roll out dough into a 12" x 8" rectangle. Place on an ungreased baking sheet. Prick with a fork.
3. Bake in preheated oven 15 minutes or until golden brown. Remove from baking sheet; cool on a wire rack.
4. Immediately before serving, preheat oven to 450F (230C). In a medium bowl, beat egg whites until soft peaks form. Gradually beat in sugar; beat until stiff and glossy.
5. Invert frozen filling onto center of cooled pastry; remove pan and paper. Spread meringue over frozen filling, sealing meringue to pastry.
6. Bake in preheated oven 5 minutes or until lightly browned. Sprinkle with chopped pistachios; serve immediately. Makes 8 servings.

Chocolate Rounds

2 oz. semisweet chocolate

1. Melt chocolate in a small heavy saucepan over very low heat. Spread melted chocolate 1/8 inch thick on waxed paper or foil.
2. When chocolate starts to harden, cut out circles with a 1- to 2-inch metal pastry cutter. Let stand until firm.
3. Gently lift rounds from paper or foil with a spatula. Place in an airtight container with waxed paper between layers. Store in a cool place until needed. Use for Mocha & Chestnut Cheesecake Roll, opposite.

Top to bottom: Cheesecake Alaska, Mocha & Chestnut Cheesecake Roll

Raspberry Bagatelle

1 baked 10-inch Genoise Sponge, page 11
3 tablespoons water
1/3 cup sugar
3 tablespoons raspberry brandy

Filling:
2 (1/4-oz.) envelopes unflavored gelatin (2 tablespoons)
1/2 cup milk
2 (8-oz.) pkgs. Neufchâtel cheese or cream cheese, room temperature
2/3 cup sugar
4 eggs, separated
2/3 cup whipping cream
3 tablespoons raspberry brandy
1 pint fresh raspberries

To decorate:
Powdered sugar
Geranium leaves or mint leaves, if desired

1. Line side of a 10-inch springform pan with waxed paper. Cut Genoise horizontally into 2 layers. Place 1 layer, cut-side up, in lined pan. Set remaining layer aside.
2. In a small saucepan over medium heat, combine water and sugar. Cook, stirring, until sugar dissolves and mixture comes to a boil. Boil 1 minute. Cool slightly. Stir in brandy. Sprinkle 1/2 of syrup over cake in pan; set aside.
3. To make filling, in a small saucepan, combine gelatin and milk. Stir well; let stand 3 minutes. Stir over low heat until gelatin dissolves; cool to room temperature.
4. In a large bowl, beat cheese and sugar until light and fluffy. Beat in egg yolks, 1 at a time, beating well after each addition. Beat in cream and brandy until blended. Beat in cooled gelatin.
5. In a medium bowl, beat egg whites until stiff but not dry. Fold beaten egg whites into cheese mixture.
6. Spread 1/4 of filling over cake in pan. Set aside a few raspberries for decoration. Arrange remaining raspberries around edge of filling. Pour remaining filling over raspberries; smooth top. Place remaining cake layer, cut-side down, on top of cheese filling. Sprinkle with remaining 1/2 of syrup. Refrigerate several hours or overnight.
7. To serve, remove side of pan; carefully peel off lining paper around side of cheesecake. Place cheesecake on a serving plate. Sift powdered sugar over top. Decorate with reserved raspberries and leaves, if desired. Makes 10 to 12 servings.

Left to right: Raspberry Bagatelle, Summer-Pudding Cheesecake

Summer-Pudding Cheesecake

1 loaf unsliced homemade-style white bread

Filling:
**3-1/4 cups fresh or frozen thawed raspberries or red
    currants or a combination of both**
2 cups pitted dark sweet cherries
2/3 cup water
2/3 cup sugar

Topping:
1/2 (8-oz.) pkg. cream cheese, room temperature
1-1/2 teaspoons grated lemon peel
1-1/2 tablespoons kirsch
1/4 cup sugar
1/2 cup whipping cream

To decorate:
Fresh red currants with stems, if desired

1. Line an 8" x 4" loaf pan completely with plastic wrap, extending wrap 1 inch above edges. Remove and discard crusts from bread. Cut bread into 3/4-inch slices. Use slices to line bottom and sides of prepared pan, trimming where necessary. Reserve enough slices to cover top.
2. To make filling, in a large saucepan, combine raspberries or currants, cherries, water and sugar. Cook over medium heat, stirring, until sugar dissolves. Pour fruit into a sieve, reserving juice. Cool fruit and juice to room temperature.
3. Brush bread in pan with cooled juice, soaking bread well.
4. Spoon cooled fruit into soaked bread-lined pan; arrange reserved bread slices over fruit. Brush top slices with more juice; there will be excess juice.
5. Place a piece of plastic wrap over pan; top with another loaf pan. Set 3 (1-pound) cans in loaf pan. Refrigerate 8 hours or overnight.
6. To make topping, in a medium bowl, beat cream cheese until fluffy; beat in lemon peel, kirsch and sugar. In a small bowl, beat whipping cream until soft peaks form. Fold whipped cream into cream-cheese mixture.
7. Remove pan and plastic wrap; invert summer pudding onto a serving plate. Remove pan and plastic wrap. Spread topping over sides and top of pudding. Refrigerate until chilled.
8. Arrange red currants in center of pudding, if desired. Makes 6 servings.

Variation
Cranberry Summer Pudding: This is a winter version of summer pudding. Substitute 2 cups fresh cranberries, 3 (2-inch) orange-peel-strips, 1-1/4 cups water, 1 cup sugar, 2 tablespoons grated orange peel and 3 cups thawed frozen raspberries for the filling above. In a large saucepan over medium heat, combine cranberries, orange peel and water. Bring to a boil. Simmer 3 to 4 minutes or until cranberries start to pop. Stir in sugar and orange peel; stir until sugar dissolves. Stir in raspberries with any juice. Cool to room temperature. Pour fruit through a sieve, reserving juice. Remove and discard orange-peel strips. Use fruit and reserved juice as directed above.

Pistachio Diplomat

About 24 ladyfingers

Pistachio Filling:
1 (8-oz.) pkg. cream cheese, room temperature
2/3 cup powdered sugar, sifted
3 tablespoons Cointreau
1/2 pint dairy sour cream (1 cup)
1/2 cup whipping cream
1 cup chopped pistachios or hazelnuts

To decorate:
Whipped cream
Julienned lemon peel
Ribbon, if desired

1. Line bottom and sides of a 9" x 5" loaf pan with waxed paper. Trim ladyfingers to fit pan. Line sides of pan with ladyfingers, reserving remaining ladyfingers for top.
2. In a medium bowl, beat cream cheese and powdered sugar until fluffy. Beat in Cointreau.
3. In a small bowl, beat sour cream to lighten. In a small bowl, beat whipping cream until soft peaks form. Fold sour cream, whipped cream and nuts into cream-cheese mixture.
4. Carefully pour mixture into lined pan. Arrange reserved ladyfingers over filling. Freeze 8 hours or until firm.
5. About 45 minutes before serving, turn out diplomat on a serving plate.
6. Spoon dollops of whipped cream down center of diplomat; sprinkle lemon peel over cream. Refrigerate 30 minutes; serve. Tie with ribbon immediately before serving, if desired. Makes 8 servings.

Strawberry-Cheesecake Crepes

1 (8-oz.) pkg. cream cheese, room temperature
1 (3-oz.) pkg. cream cheese, room temperature
3 eggs, separated
3/4 cup sugar
2 tablespoons cornstarch
1 tablespoon grated orange peel
1 tablespoon Cointreau
3 cups sliced fresh strawberries
12 cooked Dessert Crepes, page 11

To decorate:
Fresh strawberries, halved
Whipped cream, if desired

1. Preheat oven to 425F (220C). Grease a 15" x 10" baking pan. In a medium bowl, beat cream cheese, egg yolks, sugar and cornstarch until fluffy. Beat in orange peel and Cointreau. In a medium bowl, beat egg whites until stiff but not dry; fold into cream-cheese mixture.
2. Divide cream-cheese mixture among crepes, spooning mixture into center of flat crepes. Top each crepe with 1/4 cup strawberries. Roll up crepes. Lay filled crepes, seam-side down, in greased baking dish.
3. Bake in preheated oven 10 to 15 minutes or until heated through. Serve immediately with strawberry halves and whipped cream, if desired. Makes 6 servings.

Peach Cheesecake

1 recipe Sweet Shortcrust Pastry, page 8

Filling:
1/2 cup ground almonds
1-1/2 lb. fresh peaches, sliced, or 1 (29-oz.) can sliced peaches, drained
1 (8-oz.) pkg. cream cheese, room temperature
2 (3-oz.) pkgs. cream cheese, room temperature
2/3 cup sugar
1 teaspoon grated lemon peel
1 teaspoon lemon juice
1/2 cup dairy sour cream
4 eggs, separated

To decorate:
Powdered sugar

1. Prepare and bake pastry blind in a 10-inch springform pan as directed on page 8.
2. Preheat oven to 325F (165C). To make filling, sprinkle ground almonds evenly over pastry bottom in pan; press to firm slightly.
3. Arrange sliced peaches on almonds, placing them tightly together.
4. In a medium bowl, beat cream cheese, sugar, lemon peel and lemon juice until fluffy. Beat in sour cream and egg yolks.
5. In a medium bowl, beat egg whites until stiff but not dry; fold beaten egg whites into cream-cheese mixture. Pour filling over peaches; smooth top.
6. Bake in preheated oven 1 hour 20 minutes or until a wooden pick inserted off center comes out clean. Let cool in pan on a wire rack. Refrigerate until served.
7. To serve, remove side of pan. Place on a serving plate; sift powdered sugar over cheesecake. Makes 14 servings.

Left to right: Pistachio Diplomat, Strawberry-Cheesecake Crepes

Topfen Torte

1 recipe Sweet Shortcrust Pastry, page 8

Cheese Filling:
6 tablespoons butter or margarine, room temperature
3 eggs, separated
1/2 cup sugar
1 teaspoon vanilla extract
1-1/2 (8-oz.) pkgs. cream cheese, room temperature

Topping:
6 eggs, separated
1/2 cup butter or margarine, melted
1/2 cup sugar
1/2 cup all-purpose flour, sifted

To decorate:
Powdered sugar

---

1. Preheat oven to 400F (205C). Grease a 10-inch spring-form pan. On a lightly floured surface, roll out pastry to a 14-inch circle. Use pastry to line bottom and side of greased pan. Prick pastry with a fork.
2. Bake in preheated oven 15 minutes or until golden. Cool in pan on a wire rack. Reduce oven temperature to 350F (175C).
3. To make filling, in a medium bowl, beat butter or margarine with egg yolks until pale and fluffy. Beat in sugar, vanilla and cream cheese.
4. In a medium bowl, beat egg whites until stiff but not dry. Fold beaten egg whites into cream-cheese mixture. Pour mixture into cooled pastry in pan; smooth top.
5. To make topping, in a medium bowl, beat egg whites until stiff but not dry. In a small bowl, slightly beat egg yolks; fold beaten egg yolks into beaten egg whites, a little at a time.
6. Fold in 1/3 of butter or margarine; fold in 1/3 of sugar. Repeat with remaining butter or margarine and sugar. Sift flour over mixture; fold in flour.
7. Pour topping into pan over filling; smooth top.
8. Bake in preheated oven 1 hour to 1 hour 15 minutes or until puffed and golden brown. Cool in pan on a wire rack. Refrigerate until served.
9. To serve, sift powdered sugar over top. Makes 14 servings.

Borekias

Filling:
2 (8-oz.) pkgs. cream cheese, room temperature
1/4 cup honey
2 tablespoons sugar
1 teaspoon ground cinnamon

Pastry:
1 lb. filo dough (20 sheets), thawed if frozen
1 cup butter or margarine, melted

Syrup:
1 cup honey
1 cup water
1 tablespoon orange-flower water

These classic Middle Eastern pastries are modern-day relatives of original cheesecakes. Orange-flower water may be found in gourmet shops, drugstores or liquor stores.

1. Preheat oven to 325F (165C). Brush a 9-inch-square baking pan with butter or margarine.
2. To make filling, in a medium bowl, beat cream cheese, honey, sugar and cinnamon until light and fluffy. Set aside.
3. Unfold filo sheets; cover with a slightly damp towel.
4. Lay 1 filo sheet in buttered pan; brush with butter or margarine. Fold in edges to fit pan. Repeat with 9 more sheets, buttering and folding sheets to fit.
5. Spread filling over filo sheets in pan. Place a filo sheet over filling. Brush with butter or margarine. Fold in edges to fit; repeat with remaining filo sheets and butter or margarine.
6. With a knife, cut top filo sheets lengthwise into 2-1/4-inch strips. Cut diagonally across strips to make diamond shapes.
7. Bake in preheated oven 30 minutes. Increase oven temperature to 450F (230C). Bake 15 minutes or until puffed and golden brown.
8. Meanwhile, make syrup. To make syrup, in a medium saucepan over medium heat, combine honey and water. Cook, stirring, until honey dissolves. Simmer until syrup is thick enough to coat back of a spoon. Stir in orange-flower water.
9. Pour hot syrup over baked borekias immediately after removing from oven. Let cool completely in pan on a wire rack. Cut along scored lines. Serve same day as made. Makes about 16 pieces.

Cheese-Filled Brandy Snaps

Brandy Snaps:
1/2 cup butter or margarine
1/2 cup sugar
1/2 cup light corn syrup
3/4 cup all-purpose flour
1/2 teaspoon ground ginger
1/4 teaspoon ground allspice
1 teaspoon brandy

Filling:
1 (8-oz.) pkg. cream cheese or Neufchâtel, room
  temperature
3/4 cup whipping cream
1/3 cup sugar
1 teaspoon ground ginger
1 to 2 teaspoons grated lemon peel

To decorate:
Chopped candied orange peel

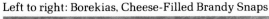

1. Preheat oven to 325F (165C). Grease and flour 2 or 3 baking sheets.
2. In a small saucepan over low heat, combine butter or margarine, sugar and corn syrup. Cook, stirring, until mixture is smooth. Cool slightly.
3. Sift flour, ginger and allspice over butter mixture; beat in with a wooden spoon until blended. Stir in brandy.
4. Drop mixture by heaping teaspoons about 4 inches apart on prepared baking sheets. Spread each cookie into a 3-inch circle.
5. Bake, 1 sheet at a time, in preheated oven 8 to 10 minutes or until golden brown. Cool on baking sheet 1 minute. Remove 1 cookie at a time with a wide flat spatula; wrap cookie around handle of a wooden spoon or cannoli tube. Let cool; slide off spoon or tube. Repeat with remaining cookies. If cookies harden before rolling, return to oven 1 minute to soften.
6. To make filling, in a medium bowl, beat cheese until light and fluffy. In a medium bowl, beat whipping cream until soft peaks form. Beat in sugar and ginger. Gradually fold whipped-cream mixture into beaten cheese. Fold in lemon peel; refrigerate until needed.
7. To serve, spoon mixture into a pastry bag fitted with a large open-star tip. Pipe cream mixture into cooled brandy snaps, filling each cookie completely. Decorate filling with candied orange peel. Serve immediately. Makes 24 cookies.

Left to right: Borekias, Cheese-Filled Brandy Snaps

Chocolate & Orange Roll

1/2 recipe Sponge Layer, page 10
2 tablespoons sugar

Grand-Marnier Filling:
1 (8-oz.) pkg. cream cheese, room temperature
1 tablespoon grated lemon peel
3 tablespoons Grand Marnier
1/3 cup sugar
3/4 cup whipping cream
1/4 cup chopped candied orange peel

To decorate:
4 oz. semisweet chocolate, chopped
Candied orange peel
Toasted sliced almonds

If desired, prepare a full recipe of Sponge Layers; bake in two pans. Freeze one layer, unfilled, to use later.

1. Preheat oven to 425F (220C). Line a 13" x 9" baking pan with waxed paper, extending paper 2 inches above pan on all sides. Grease paper. Prepare sponge-layer batter as directed on page 10. Pour sponge-layer batter into pan; smooth top.
2. Bake in preheated oven 10 to 15 minutes or until center springs back when lightly pressed.
3. Place a clean towel on a flat surface; sprinkle with sugar. Invert cake onto sugared towel; remove pan. Carefully peel off paper. Trim edges of cake. Starting from 1 short end, roll up cake and towel. Completely cool rolled cake on a wire rack.
4. To make filling, in a medium bowl, beat cream cheese until fluffy; beat in lemon peel, Grand Marnier and sugar. In a small bowl, beat whipping cream until soft peaks form. Fold whipped cream and orange peel into cream-cheese mixture.
5. Unroll cake; spread filling over cake to within 1/2 inch of edges. Reroll cake without towel; place, seam-side down, on a serving plate.
6. Melt chocolate in a small heavy saucepan over very low heat; stir until smooth. Pour warm melted chocolate over roll; smooth with a small spatula that has been dipped in hot water. Decorate top of roll with candied orange peel and almonds. Refrigerate until served or up to 6 hours. Makes 6 servings.

Apricot Vacherin

1 recipe Grand-Marnier Filling, from Chocolate & Orange Roll, opposite
1 baked 9-inch Meringue Layer, from Lemon Japonais, page 50
3 tablespoons red-currant jelly
1 (29-oz.) can apricot halves, drained

To decorate:
2 tablespoons chopped pistachios

1. Prepare filling as directed opposite.
2. Spread meringue with jelly. Reserve 4 apricot halves for decoration; arrange remaining apricot halves over jelly-covered meringue. Carefully spread filling over apricots.
3. Cut reserved apricot halves in half. Arrange apricot quarters in a circle around center of vacherin; sprinkle pistachios in center of apricot ring.
4. Refrigerate 1 hour. Makes 10 servings.

Left to right: Apricot Vacherin, Cheese-Filled Chocolate Brownies, Chocolate & Orange Roll

Cheese-Filled Chocolate Brownies

Filling:
1 (8-oz.) pkg. cream cheese, room temperature
2 tablespoons butter or margarine, room temperature
1/2 cup sugar
1 teaspoon vanilla extract
1 egg
1/4 cup all-purpose flour

Brownie Mixture:
4 oz. semisweet chocolate, chopped
3 tablespoons butter or margarine
2 eggs
3/4 cup sugar
2 tablespoons all-purpose flour
1/2 teaspoon baking powder
Pinch of salt
1/4 teaspoon almond extract
1 cup chopped pecans or toasted hazelnuts

1. Preheat oven to 350F (175C). Grease an 8-inch-square pan. To make filling, in a medium bowl, beat cream cheese and butter or margarine until light and fluffy. Beat in sugar, vanilla, egg and flour until blended. Set aside.
2. To make brownie layer, melt chocolate and butter or margarine in a small heavy saucepan over low heat. Stir until smooth; cool to room temperature.
3. In a medium bowl, beat eggs and sugar until thick and lemon-colored. Beat in cooled chocolate mixture. Sift flour, baking powder and salt into a small bowl. Gradually stir flour mixture into chocolate mixture. Stir in almond extract and 3/4 cup nuts.
4. Spread 1/2 of chocolate mixture in bottom of greased pan. Spread filling over chocolate mixture. Spread remaining chocolate mixture over filling.
5. Draw a knife through mixture with a zigzag motion to make a marbled effect; sprinkle with remaining nuts.
6. Bake in preheated oven 35 to 40 minutes or until firm to the touch.
7. Cut into 16 squares while still warm. Cool in pan on a wire rack. Makes 16 squares.

Turotorta

1-1/4 cups sifted all-purpose flour
1 tablespoon granulated sugar
5 tablespoons butter or margarine
1 egg yolk
2/3 cup dairy sour cream
1 (8-oz.) pkg. cream cheese, room temperature
1 cup granulated sugar
6 eggs, separated
1 teaspoon vanilla extract
1 tablespoon grated orange peel
Powdered sugar

---

1. Preheat oven to 425F (220C). Remove side of a 9-inch springform pan; grease bottom of pan.
2. In a medium bowl, combine flour and 1 tablespoon granulated sugar. With a pastry blender or 2 knives, cut in butter or margarine until mixture resembles coarse crumbs. Stir in egg yolk and sour cream to make a smooth dough.

3. Divide pastry in half. Roll out 1 piece of pastry to a 9-inch circle; place on greased pan bottom. Prick pastry with a fork. Set remaining pastry aside.
4. Bake rolled-out pastry in preheated oven 8 to 10 minutes or until golden. Cool completely on bottom of pan on a wire rack. When cool, fasten on side of pan; grease sides. Reduce oven temperature to 325F (165C).
5. In a large bowl, beat cream cheese and 1 cup granulated sugar until light and fluffy. Beat in 6 egg yolks, 1 at a time, beating well after each addition. Beat in vanilla and orange peel until blended.
6. In a large bowl, beat egg whites until stiff but not dry. Fold in beaten egg whites. Pour mixture over baked pastry in pan; smooth top.
7. Bake in preheated oven 20 minutes. While cheesecake is baking, roll out reserved pastry to a 9-inch circle. Place reserved pastry gently on top of baked filling. Bake 40 to 50 minutes more or until pastry is golden and puffed. Cool in pan on a wire rack 2 hours.
8. Refrigerate until served. To serve, run a knife around inside edge of pan. Carefully remove side of pan; place cheesecake on a serving plate. Immediately before serving, sift powdered sugar over cheesecake. Makes 10 to 12 servings.

Left to right: Turotorta, Russian Paskha

Russian Paskha

1 cup unsalted butter or margarine, room temperature
1 cup sugar
2 eggs
1-1/2 cups cottage cheese, well drained
1 (8-oz.) pkg. cream cheese, room temperature
1/2 cup whipping cream
1 cup chopped toasted almonds
2 tablespoons chopped pistachios
2/3 cup raisins
2 tablespoons chopped candied orange peel
2 tablespoons chopped candied lemon peel
1 teaspoon vanilla extract or 1/2 teaspoon rose water

To decorate:
Toasted almonds
Candied-cherry halves
Angelica strips

This traditional Easter dessert is usually set in a pyramid-shaped wooden mold which has the imprint of the Russian Orthodox cross on one of its faces. A well-scrubbed, new clay flowerpot, 6 inches wide and 5-1/2 inches deep, can be used. Line it with muslin or cheesecloth as follows. Place a large sheet of muslin or cheesecloth over pot; cut a slit from one edge to center. Push cloth into pot, overlapping cut edges. Smooth cloth against sides. Make sure that piece is large enough to leave an edge which can be folded over top of filled flowerpot. This cheesecake is very rich and should be served in small portions.

1. Line a mold or flowerpot as directed above. In a large bowl, beat butter or margarine and sugar until pale and fluffy; beat in eggs, 1 at a time, beating well after each addition.
2. Press cottage cheese through a sieve into egg mixture; beat in until blended. Beat in cream cheese until blended. Beat in whipping cream.
3. Stir in almonds, pistachios, raisins, candied peels and vanilla or rose water.
4. Pour mixture into lined mold; fold over edges of cloth to cover filling. Lay a small plate or saucer over filling. Set a 2-pound weight on top.
5. Set mold or flowerpot on a small rack in a pan to catch any liquid that drains out. Refrigerate 8 to 10 hours.
6. To serve, remove weight and plate; uncover top. Invert onto a serving plate; remove mold or flowerpot. Carefully peel off cloth. Decorate with almonds, candied-cherry halves and angelica. Makes 15 servings.

Polish Cheesecake

1 Sweet Shortcrust Pastry, page 8
Filling:
2 teaspoons grated lemon peel
1/3 cup raisins
1 tablespoon dark rum
1 tablespoon white wine
Pinch of saffron threads
1 cup sugar
2 tablespoons cold water
3/4 cup ground almonds
2 (8-oz.) pkgs. Neufchâtel cheese or cream cheese, room temperature
5 egg yolks
2 tablespoons sliced almonds

To decorate:
Powdered sugar

Saffron has a very distinctive flavor. It gives a rich golden tint to this cheesecake.

1. Prepare and bake pastry blind in a 9-inch springform pan as directed on page 8.
2. Preheat oven to 400F (205C). To make filling, in a small bowl, combine lemon peel, raisins and rum. In another small bowl, combine white wine and saffron. Let both mixtures stand 2 hours. Add raisin-and-rum mixture to wine mixture. Set aside.
3. In a small heavy saucepan over low heat, combine 1/2 cup sugar and water. Cook, stirring, until sugar dissolves. Bring to a boil. Boil, without stirring, to thread stage 230F (110C) on a candy thermometer. Remove from heat. Quickly stir in ground almonds. Return to heat; stir until mixture thickens. Spread warm mixture in baked pastry shell.
4. In a medium bowl, beat cheese until light and fluffy. Beat in egg yolks, 1 at a time, beating well after each addition. Beat in remaining 1/2 cup sugar until combined. Beat in raisin mixture.
5. Spread cheese filling evenly over almond mixture; sprinkle with sliced almonds.
6. Bake in preheated oven 1 hour or until puffed and golden brown. Cool on a wire rack. Refrigerate until served. Immediately before serving, sift powdered sugar over top. Makes 8 servings.

Savory Cheesecakes

Vegetable & Cheese Terrine

1 cup cottage cheese, drained, sieved
2 (3-oz.) pkgs. cream cheese, room temperature
1/2 cup dairy sour cream
3 egg yolks
1/2 teaspoon salt
1/2 teaspoon freshly ground pepper
1/2 bunch watercress
10 small carrots
1 cup small fresh or frozen green peas
2 small zucchini
1 cup chopped green beans
1 lemon, peeled, thinly sliced
1 recipe Savory Crumb Base, from Avocado-Cheese Ring with Shrimp, page 75

To garnish:
Fresh parsley

To serve:
Chilled Tomato Sauce, below

Here is a spectacular hors d'oeuvre for a special dinner party. The subtle flavor of the smooth cheese-and-watercress filling compliments the crisp vegetables.

1. In a large bowl, beat cottage cheese and cream cheese until combined; stir in sour cream and egg yolks. Add salt and pepper; set aside.
2. In a blender or food processor with a steel blade, process watercress until pureed. Spoon 1/3 of cheese mixture into a medium bowl; stir in watercress puree. Refrigerate watercress-cheese mixture and remaining cheese mixture 30 minutes.
3. Steam carrots, peas, zucchini and green beans until crisp-tender. Drain; rinse under cold running water to stop cooking. Cool to room temperature.
4. Preheat oven to 350F (175C). Cut steamed zucchini in quarters lengthwise.
5. Lightly oil a 12" x 4 " terrine; line with waxed paper. Arrange lemon slices in a row in center of pan bottom.
6. Spread 1/3 of plain cheese mixture over lemon slices. Arrange a row of zucchini quarters lengthwise on top of cheese mixture. Spread another 1/3 of cheese mixture over zucchini quarters. Cover cheese mixture with a layer of peas. Spread peas with remaining 1/3 of cheese mixture. Arrange cooled green beans lengthwise over cheese mixture.

7. Cover beans with 1/2 of watercress-cheese mixture. Arrange carrots lengthwise over watercress mixture. Spread remaining 1/2 of watercress-cheese mixture over carrots.
8. Prepare crumb base as directed on page 75. Press crumb mixture on top of watercress-cheese mixture. Cover tightly with a lid or foil. Place covered terrine in a roasting pan. Add enough boiling water to almost fill roasting pan.
9. Bake in preheated oven 45 minutes or until top starts to crack.
10. Remove lid or foil; cool on a wire rack; refrigerate overnight. Invert on a long flat serving plate; remove pan and paper. Garnish with fresh cilantro or parsley. To serve, cut into slices; serve with Chilled Tomato Sauce. Makes 12 servings.

Chilled Tomato Sauce

2 (28-oz.) cans tomatoes, drained
1 teaspoon sugar
1 tablespoon tomato paste
2 tablespoons white-wine vinegar
6 tablespoons olive oil
1 teaspoon salt
1/2 teaspoon freshly ground pepper
1 tablespoon chopped fresh tarragon or 1 teaspoon dried leaf tarragon

1. In a blender or food processor with a steel blade, process tomatoes until pureed. Press through a sieve into a medium bowl; discard seeds. Refrigerate until chilled.
2. Return tomato puree to blender or food processor; add sugar, tomato paste and vinegar. Process a few seconds or until combined. With machine motor running, slowly add olive oil to mixture. Process until smooth and thick.
3. Season with salt and pepper. Stir in tarragon. Refrigerate until served. Makes about 7 cups.

Vegetable & Cheese Terrine with Chilled Tomato Sauce

Top to bottom: Talmouses with Brie, Fresh Goat's Cheese Flan

Fresh Goat's Cheese Flan

1 recipe Shortcrust Pastry, page 8

Filling:
2 tablespoons butter or margarine
2 tablespoons all-purpose flour
1 cup milk
1/2 teaspoon freshly ground pepper
2 egg yolks
7 oz. goat's cheese, crumbled
1/3 cup grated Parmesan cheese (1 oz.)
1/3 cup chopped cooked ham, if desired

To garnish:
Fresh coriander leaves

1. Prepare and bake pastry blind in an 8-inch flan pan as directed on page 8.
2. Preheat oven to 375F (190C). To make filling, melt butter in a medium saucepan over low heat. Stir in flour; cook 1 to 2 minutes, stirring constantly. Gradually stir in milk. Simmer mixture, stirring 5 minutes; stir in pepper and egg yolks.
3. Remove from heat; stir in cheeses. Stir until cheeses melt. Stir in ham, if desired. Pour filling into pastry shell.
4. Bake in preheated oven 30 minutes or until golden brown. Cool in pan on a wire rack.
5. Serve warm or cool. Garnish with coriander leaves. Makes 8 servings.

Talmouses with Brie

1/2 (17-1/2-oz.) pkg. frozen puff pastry (1 sheet), thawed
1/2 cup milk
1/4 cup butter or margarine, diced
Pinch of salt
1/2 cup all-purpose flour
1 egg
1 egg yolk
4 oz. Brie cheese, rind removed, mashed
1 tablespoon whipping cream
To glaze:
1 egg, beaten

These light flower-like pastries are made of a delicious combination of puff pastry and Brie choux pastry.

1. Preheat oven to 375F (190C). Unfold pastry sheet. On a lightly floured surface, roll out pastry to a 15-inch square about 1/16 inch thick. With a sharp knife, cut pastry into 36 (2-1/2-inch) squares. Cover; set aside.
2. In a medium saucepan over medium heat, combine milk, butter or margarine and salt. Bring to a boil. Add flour, all at once. Stir with a wooden spoon until dough forms a ball and comes away from side of pan. Let cool slightly.
3. Beat in egg, beating well. Beat in egg yolk, beating well. Beat in cheese and cream.
4. Place 1 teaspoon of cheese mixture in center of each pastry square. Moisten edges of each square with water. Press 2 opposite sides together, leaving long edge open. Bring top corners of sealed sides together in center. Press remaining open edges together to form a square package; see illustration below.
5. Dampen a large baking sheet. Brush each package with egg to glaze; do not brush cut edges. Place packages on damp baking sheet.
6. Bake in preheated oven 30 minutes or until puffed and golden brown. Serve warm. Makes 36 pastries.

Cheese Tart

1 recipe Shortcrust Pastry, page 8
Filling:
1/4 cup butter or margarine
1/2 cup all-purpose flour
1 cup milk
2 cups shredded Cheddar cheese (8 oz.)
6 eggs, separated
1/2 teaspoon salt
1/2 teaspoon freshly ground pepper
2 tablespoons chopped fresh chives
1 tablespoon chopped fresh parsley
About 1/2 teaspoon hot-pepper sauce

This hot soufflé cheesecake is a variation of a classic French supper dish. Serve it with a crisp green salad.

1. Prepare and bake pastry blind in an 8-inch springform pan as directed on page 8. Cool on a wire rack.
2. To make filling, melt butter or margarine in a medium saucepan over low heat; stir in flour. Cook 2 to 3 minutes, stirring constantly. Gradually stir in milk. Cool slightly.
3. Beat in cheese and egg yolks, 1 at a time, beating well after each addition. Return to low heat until cheese melts. Stir in salt, pepper, chives, parsley and hot-pepper sauce to taste.
4. In a medium bowl, beat egg whites until stiff but not dry; fold beaten egg whites into cheese mixture. Pour mixture immediately into baked pastry shell.
5. Bake 30 minutes or until puffed and golden brown. Carefully remove side of pan; serve immediately. Makes 4 servings.

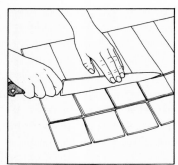

1/Cut pastry into 36 (2-1/2-inch) squares.

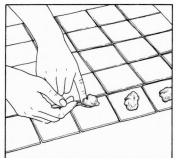

2/Place 1 teaspoon cheese mixture in center of each pastry square.

3/Moisten edges of each square with water.

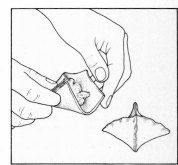

4/Press 2 opposite sides together.

Cucumber-Cheese Mousse

1 large cucumber, peeled, seeded, diced
2 teaspoons salt
3 tablespoons lemon juice
1 (1/4-oz.) envelope unflavored gelatin (1 tablespoon)
1/4 cup chicken stock
1 (8-oz.) pkg. cream cheese, room temperature
1/2 pint dairy sour cream (1 cup)
1/2 pint whipping cream (1 cup)
1/4 cup finely chopped green onions
3 tablespoons freshly chopped parsley
2 tablespoons freshly chopped chives
1/2 teaspoon white pepper
1 recipe Savory Crumb Base, from Avocado-Cheese
   Ring with Shrimp, page 75

To garnish:
Thin cucumber slices
Chopped chives
Parsley sprig

1. Place diced cucumber in a colander; sprinkle with salt and 1 tablespoon lemon juice. Stir well. Place a heavy plate over cucumber mixture. Place colander in a large bowl; let drain 1 hour. Press out liquid. Place cucumber between sheets of paper towels; pat dry. Set aside.
2. In a small saucepan, combine gelatin and stock. Stir well; let stand 3 minutes. Stir over low heat until gelatin dissolves; cool to room temperature. In a medium bowl, beat cream cheese until fluffy. Beat in sour cream just until blended; set aside.
3. In a medium bowl, beat whipping cream until soft peaks form. Fold reserved cucumber, green onions, parsley and chives into whipped cream. Gradually stir in cooled gelatin until blended. Add remaining 2 tablespoons lemon juice and white pepper; stir until combined.
4. Oil a 6-cup (8-inch) brioche mold; set aside. Fold cucumber mixture into cream-cheese mixture. Pour mixture into oiled mold; smooth top. Refrigerate 1 hour.
5. Prepare crumb base as directed on page 75. Press crumb mixture on top of chilled mousse. Refrigerate 2 to 3 hours or until served.
6. To serve, place a serving plate over top of mousse; invert. Rinse a towel under hot running water; wring dry. Wrap hot towel around outside of mold. Let stand 10 to 15 seconds. Carefully remove mold. Return mousse to refrigerator 15 minutes to firm up. Decorate with cucumber slices, chopped chives and a parsley sprig. Makes 8 to 12 servings.

Cucumber-Cheese Mousse

Smoked-Salmon & Cheese Mold

3 eggs, separated
1 cup milk
1 (1/4-oz.) envelope unflavored gelatin (1 tablespoon)
3 tablespoons water
1 (8-oz.) pkg. Neufchâtel cheese or cream cheese, room temperature
1 tablespoon lemon juice
1/2 teaspoon freshly ground pepper
8 oz. smoked salmon, diced
2 tablespoons minced onion
1/2 cup whipping cream
1 recipe Savory Crumb Base, from Avocado-Cheese Ring with Shrimp, page 75

To garnish:
8 pimento-stuffed olives
Smoked-salmon strips
Endive

1. Oil a 1-quart fish-shaped mold. Combine egg yolks and milk in a medium bowl over a pan of simmering water. Cook, stirring, until mixture thickens. Place bowl in a pan or sink of cold water to cool slightly.
2. In a small saucepan, combine gelatin and water. Stir well; let stand 3 minutes. Stir over low heat until gelatin dissolves; cool to room temperature. Beat cheese, lemon juice and pepper into cooled egg mixture. Stir in cooled gelatin. Fold in smoked salmon and onion; refrigerate until mixture mounds when dropped from a spoon.
3. In a medium bowl, beat egg whites until stiff but not dry. Fold beaten egg whites into chilled mixture. In a medium bowl, beat cream until soft peaks form; fold into chilled mixture.
4. Pour mixture into oiled mold; refrigerate 1 hour. Prepare crumb base as directed on page 75. Press crumb mixture on top of chilled mold. Refrigerate 3 to 4 hours or until served.
5. To serve, place a serving plate over top of mold; invert. Rinse a towel under hot running water; wring dry. Wrap hot towel around outside of mold. Let stand 10 to 15 seconds. Carefully remove mold. Return to refrigerator 15 minutes to firm up. Garnish with stuffed olives, smoked salmon and endive. Makes 8 servings.

Spicy Vegetable Mold

1 (1/4-oz.) envelope unflavored gelatin (1 tablespoon)
1/2 cup water
1/2 cup prepared taco sauce
1/2 pint dairy sour cream (1 cup)
2 cups shredded Monterey Jack cheese (8 oz.)
1 (4-oz.) can diced green chilies, drained
1/2 cup cooked or canned whole-kernel corn, drained
1 green onion, finely chopped
1 celery stalk, finely chopped
Garlic powder

To garnish:
Ripe olives, sliced

To serve:
Tortilla chips
Jicama slices

1. In a small saucepan, combine gelatin and water. Stir well; let stand 3 minutes. Stir over low heat until gelatin dissolves; cool to room temperature. Stir in taco sauce.
2. In a medium bowl, combine sour cream, cheese, chilies, corn, green onion and celery. Season with garlic powder. Stir in cooled gelatin mixture.
3. Refrigerate until mixture mounds when dropped from a spoon. Oil a 4-cup mold. Stir gelatin mixture to distribute ingredients. Spoon into oiled mold. Refrigerate 4 to 5 hours or until firm.
4. To serve, place a serving plate over top of mold; invert. Rinse a towel under hot running water; wring dry. Wrap hot towel around outside of mold. Let stand 10 to 15 seconds. Carefully remove mold. Return to refrigerator 15 minutes to firm up. Garnish with olives. Serve with tortilla chips and jicama slices. Makes about 4 cups.

Hot Swiss-Cheese Tarts

1 recipe Shortcrust Pastry, page 8

Filling:
1-3/4 cups shredded Swiss cheese (7 oz.)
2 eggs, beaten
1/2 cup milk
1/2 cup whipping cream
Pinch of nutmeg
1/2 teaspoon white pepper
1/2 teaspoon salt

To garnish:
Red (cayenne) pepper or paprika
Fresh parsley sprigs

These tarts are an unusual appetizer to serve with drinks.

1. Preheat oven to 375F (190C). Grease 12 deep 2-1/2- to 3-inch tart pans. Prepare pastry as directed on page 8. On a lightly floured surface, roll out pastry to 1/4 inch thick. Cut circles about 1/2 inch larger than pans. Use pastry to line greased tart pans. Prick pastry all over with a fork. Refrigerate until chilled.
2. Sprinkle 1/2 of cheese into chilled pastry-lined pans.
3. In a bowl, combine remaining cheese, eggs, milk, cream, nutmeg, white pepper and salt. Blend well. Ladle mixture over cheese.
4. Bake in preheated oven 20 minutes or until a knife inserted off center comes out clean.
5. Sprinkle each tart with a little red pepper or paprika. Place a parsley sprig on each tart; remove from pans. Serve immediately. Makes about 12 tarts.

Cheese & Spinach Cornets

1 tablespoon butter or margarine
2 tablespoons finely chopped shallots
1/2 cup grated Parmesan cheese (2 oz.)
1 (10-oz.) pkg. thawed frozen chopped spinach, drained
1/2 (8-oz.) pkg. cream cheese, room temperature
Pinch of nutmeg
1/2 teaspoon salt
1/2 teaspoon freshly ground pepper
1 egg yolk
12 cooked Basic Crepes, page 11

1. Preheat oven to 425F (220C). Grease a 15" x 10" baking pan. Melt butter or margarine in a medium skillet over low heat. Add shallots; sauté until soft, stirring occasionally. Set aside.
2. Reserve 1 tablespoon Parmesan cheese. In a medium bowl, beat remaining Parmesan cheese, spinach and cream cheese until combined. Stir in sautéed shallots, nutmeg, salt and pepper. Stir in egg yolk.

3. Spoon 1/12th of filling on 1/4 of 1 crepe. Fold crepe in half with filling at 1 side of fold. Beginning at filled section, roll into a cornet shape. Place in greased pan. Prepare 11 more cornets in same way. Sprinkle reserved Parmesan cheese on top.
4. Bake in preheated oven 10 to 15 minutes or until heated through.
5. Carefully remove from pan; serve hot. Makes 4 to 6 servings.

Cheese & Spinach Filo Rolls

1 (8-oz) pkg. cream cheese, room temperature
1/2 teaspoon salt
1/2 teaspoon freshly ground pepper
1 egg, beaten
1/2 teaspoon grated nutmeg
1 (10-oz.) pkg. thawed frozen chopped spinach, drained
2 tablespoons pine nuts
6 filo-dough sheets, thawed if frozen
1/2 cup butter or margarine, melted

1. Preheat oven to 375F (190C). Grease a large baking sheet. In a medium bowl, beat cheese until light and fluffy. Beat in salt, pepper, egg, nutmeg and spinach. Stir in pine nuts.
2. Unfold filo sheets; place on a flat surface. Cover filo with a slightly damp towel. Cut a filo sheet into 4 long strips about 3 inches wide. Brush strips with melted butter or margarine. Place a heaping teaspoon of filling at end of 1 strip; fold end over filling. See photograph page 9.
3. Fold in long sides of pastry; fold over filled end again and again to form a square package. Repeat with remaining filo strips. Cut remaining filo sheets into strips; fill and roll strips, making a total of 24 rolled packages.
4. Brush each package with melted butter or margarine; arrange 1/2 inch apart on greased baking sheet.
5. Bake in preheated oven 10 minutes or until golden brown.
6. Serve warm with drinks. Makes 24 appetizers.

Clockwise from left: Cheese & Spinach Filo Rolls, Hot Swiss-Cheese Tarts, Cheese & Spinach Cornets

Herb & Cheese Strudel

2 tablespoons butter or margarine
2 tablespoons chopped fresh parsley
2 tablespoons chopped chives
1 teaspoon dried leaf chervil
2 tablespoons toasted bread crumbs
2 (8-oz.) pkgs. cream cheese, room temperature
2 egg yolks
1/2 cup dairy sour cream
1 teaspoon salt
8 oz. filo dough (10 sheets), thawed if frozen
1/2 cup butter or margarine, melted
8 oz. small green beans, cooked, or 1 (8-oz.) can green beans, drained

1. Preheat oven to 400F (205C). Grease a large baking sheet. Melt 2 tablespoons butter or margarine in a medium skillet over low heat. Add herbs and bread crumbs. Cook, stirring, 2 minutes. Cool to room temperature.
2. In a medium bowl, beat cream cheese until light and fluffy. Beat in egg yolks, sour cream and salt. Stir in cooled crumb mixture.
3. Unfold filo sheets; cover with a slightly damp towel. Place a dry towel on a flat surface. Lay 1 filo sheet on towel; brush with melted butter or margarine. Place another filo sheet next to first sheet, overlapping edges by 2-1/2 inches. Brush second sheet with melted butter or margarine. Top with remaining 8 filo sheets, arranging in same way. Brush each 1 with melted butter or margarine.
4. Spread filling over filo to within 1 inch of edges. Arrange beans crosswise over filling.
5. Fold edges of pastry over filling. Using towel and starting from 1 short end, roll up filled pastry.
6. Use towel to place strudel, seam-side down, on greased baking sheet. Brush strudel with melted butter or margarine.
7. Bake in preheated oven 40 minutes or until puffed and golden brown. Serve hot. Makes 6 to 8 servings.

Left to right: Herb & Cheese Strudel, Curried-Seafood & Cheese Crepes

Curried-Seafood & Cheese Crepes

12 cooked Basic Crepes, page 11

Seafood Filling:
1 tablespoon finely chopped fresh parsley
1 teaspoon curry powder
1/2 teaspoon hot-pepper sauce
1 tablespoon tomato paste
2 medium tomatoes, chopped
8 oz. cooked, flaked fish (about 1-1/2 cups)
8 oz. deveined, peeled, cooked shrimp (about 2 cups)
1 teaspoon salt
1/2 teaspoon freshly ground pepper

Cheese Filling:
1 (8-oz.) pkg. cream cheese, room temperature
1 (3-oz.) pkg. cream cheese, room temperature
3 eggs, separated
1/2 teaspoon freshly ground pepper

To garnish:
2 tablespoons grated Parmesan cheese
24 deveined, peeled, cooked shrimp
Fresh parsley sprigs

Choose the type of fish according to availability. Turbot, haddock, hake and salmon are all equally delicious in this recipe.

1. Reserve crepes. Preheat oven to 425F (220C). Grease a 15" x 10" baking pan. To make seafood filling, in a medium saucepan, combine parsley, curry powder, hot-pepper sauce, tomato paste and tomatoes. Simmer 5 minutes. Stir in fish and shrimp. Season with salt and pepper; set aside.

2. To make cheese filling, in a medium bowl, beat cream cheese, egg yolks and pepper until light and fluffy. In a medium bowl, beat egg whites until stiff but not dry. Fold in beaten egg whites.

3. To fill crepes, spoon 1/12 of seafood filling onto a crepe, just off center. Spoon 1/12 of cheese filling next to seafood filling; roll up. Place filled crepe, seam-side down, in greased baking pan. Repeat with remaining crepes and filling. Sprinkle crepes with Parmesan cheese.

4. Bake in preheated oven 10 to 15 minutes or until cheese filling is set.

5. To serve, carefully remove crepes; garnish with parsley and shrimp. Makes 6 servings.

Spinach & Cheese-Filled Soufflé Rolls

Soufflé:
1/2 cup butter or margarine
1/2 cup all-purpose flour
2-1/4 cups milk
1/2 teaspoon salt
Freshly ground pepper
8 eggs, separated
1 cup shredded Cheddar cheese (4 oz.)

Filling:
1 tablespoon butter or margarine
2 tablespoons finely chopped shallots
3 cups finely chopped mushrooms (about 6 oz.)
1 cup finely chopped ham
1 (10-oz.) pkg. thawed frozen chopped spinach, well drained
1 cup shredded mozzarella or Swiss cheese (4 oz.)
Pinch of nutmeg
1/2 teaspoon salt
Freshly ground pepper

Serve rolls for lunch or supper with a crisp green salad. To make three to four servings, cut everything in half; bake in one pan.

1. Preheat oven to 400F (205C). Grease 2 (15" x 10") baking pans. Line with waxed paper; grease paper.
2. To make white sauce for soufflé, melt butter or margarine in a medium saucepan over medium heat. Stir in flour; cook 2 to 3 minutes, stirring constantly. Gradually stir in milk, stirring constantly. Bring to a boil. Reduce heat; simmer 5 minutes, stirring. Season with salt and pepper. Remove from heat. Pour 1/2 of white sauce into a small bowl; reserve for filling.
3. Beat egg yolks, 1 at a time, into remaining sauce. Stir in cheese. Stir over low heat 2 to 3 minutes or until cheese melts.
4. In a medium bowl, beat egg whites until stiff but not dry; fold beaten egg whites into cheese sauce. Divide mixture between lined pans, spooning it into corners.
5. Bake 15 minutes or until golden brown.
6. Make filling while soufflés bake. To make filling, melt butter or margarine in a large skillet. Add shallots, mushrooms and ham; sauté 5 minutes, stirring. Add spinach, reserved white sauce, cheese, nutmeg, salt and pepper.
7. When soufflés are done, immediately turn out onto 2 clean towels. Peel off paper.
8. Divide warm filling between soufflés, spreading to within 1/2 inch of edges. Using towel and starting from 1 short end, roll up each filled soufflé.
9. Place filled soufflés, seam-side down, on a serving plate. Serve immediately or keep warm in turned-off oven up to 15 minutes. Makes 6 to 8 servings.

Avocado-Cheese Ring with Shrimp

2 (1/4-oz.) envelopes unflavored gelatin (2 tablespoons)
1 cup chicken broth
2 large ripe avocados
1 tablespoon finely chopped green onion
1 tablespoon Worcestershire sauce
1/2 teaspoon salt
1/2 teaspoon white pepper
1/2 teaspoon hot-pepper sauce
1 cup small-curd cottage cheese, drained
2/3 cup whipping cream
2 egg whites

Savory Crumb Base:
2 cups fresh white bread crumbs, toasted
1 to 2 tablespoons freshly chopped parsley
6 tablespoons butter or margarine, melted

To serve:
Endive leaves
1/2 to 3/4 lb. deveined, peeled, cooked shrimp

---

1. To make ring, in a small saucepan, combine gelatin and 1/2 cup broth. Stir well; let stand 3 minutes. Stir over low heat until gelatin dissolves; Remove from heat; stir in remaining 1/2 cup broth. Cool to room temperature.
2. In a blender or food processor with a steel blade, process avocados until pureed. Spoon into a medium bowl; stir in cooled gelatin mixture. Stir in green onion, Worcestershire sauce, salt, white pepper and hot-pepper sauce. Refrigerate mixture about 20 minutes or until mixture mounds when dropped from a spoon.
3. Brush a 6-1/2-cup ring mold with vegetable oil; set aside. In a blender or food processor with a steel blade, process cottage cheese until smooth. Fold pureed cottage cheese into chilled avocado mixture. In a medium bowl, beat whipped cream until soft peaks form. Fold whipped cream into avocado mixture.
4. In a medium bowl, beat egg whites until stiff but not dry. Fold beaten egg whites into avocado mixture. Pour into oiled mold; smooth top. Refrigerate 1 hour.
5. To make crumb base, in a medium bowl, combine bread crumbs, parsley and butter or margarine until blended. Press lightly onto chilled cheesecake. Refrigerate 3 to 4 hours or overnight.
6. To serve, place a serving plate over top of ring; invert. Rinse a clean towel under hot running water; wring dry. Wrap towel around outside of mold. Let stand 10 to 15 seconds. Remove ring mold. Chill in refrigerator 15 to 20 minutes to firm up. Fill center with endive leaves and shrimp. Makes 12 to 14 servings.

Left to right: Spinach & Cheese-Filled Soufflé Roll, Avocado-Cheese Ring with Shrimp

Cottage-Cheese Konafa

1 lb. konafa pastry
1 cup unsalted butter or margarine, melted
1 lb. cottage cheese (2 cups), sieved, or 2 (8-oz.) pkgs.
  Neufchâtel cheese, room temperature
1 cup shredded Cheddar cheese (4 oz.)
3 eggs, beaten
1 tablespoon dried leaf mint
1/2 teaspoon ground nutmeg
1/2 teaspoon freshly ground pepper

Serve this Middle Eastern savory cheesecake as a starter or as a light supper dish. Konafa pastry looks like soft white strands of uncooked thin spaghetti. It can be bought in Greek and Middle Eastern shops.

1. Preheat oven to 350F (175C). Place konafa pastry in a large bowl; gently pull strands apart. Pour melted butter or margarine over top; toss lightly until each strand is coated.
2. Grease a 9-inch springform pan. Firmly press 1/2 of pastry over bottom and side of greased pan.
3. To make filling, in a medium bowl, beat cottage cheese or Neufchâtel cheese, Cheddar cheese, eggs, mint, nutmeg and pepper until combined.
4. Spoon filling into pastry-lined pan. Arrange remaining pastry over filling; press down firmly.
5. Bake in preheated oven 35 minutes. Increase temperature to 450F (230C). Bake 15 minutes or until a wooden pick inserted in center comes out clean.
6. Carefully remove side of pan. Place cheesecake on a serving plate. Cut in wedges; serve hot. Makes 8 to 10 servings.

Cheese & Eggplant Flan

1 recipe Shortcrust Pastry, page 8
Filling:
1-3/4 lb. eggplant, cut crosswise into 1/4-inch slices
2-1/2 tablespoons salt
2 tablespoons olive oil
1 cup cottage cheese, drained, sieved
2 (3-oz.) pkgs. cream cheese, room temperature
3 eggs
2 tablespoons chopped fresh dill or 1 teaspoon dried dill
  weed
2 tablespoons chopped fresh basil or 1 tablespoon dried
  leaf basil
Salt
Freshly ground pepper
2 tablespoons grated Parmesan cheese

To garnish:
Fresh dill sprigs and basil

1. Prepare and bake pastry blind in an 8-inch springform pan as directed on page 8. Cool on a wire rack.
2. Arrange eggplant in a colander; sprinkle with salt. Let drain 30 minutes. Rinse; squeeze out water. Dry with paper towels.
3. Preheat broiler. Brush dried eggplant slices lightly with oil; place on a baking sheet. Broil 5 minutes on each side to soften.
4. Preheat oven to 350F (175C). In a medium bowl, blend cheeses, eggs, dill and basil. Season with salt and pepper.
5. Arrange 1/2 of broiled eggplant slices in bottom of baked pastry shell. Pour in cheese mixture; arrange remaining eggplant slices on top. Sprinkle with Parmesan cheese.
6. Bake in preheated oven 1 hour or until filling is set.
7. Remove side of pan. Place flan on a serving plate. Garnish with dill and basil. Serve hot. Makes 6 servings.

1/Gently pull strands of konafa pastry apart.

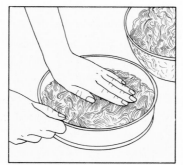

2/Firmly press 1/2 of pastry over bottom and side of greased pan.

3/Spoon filling into pastry-lined pan.

4/Arrange remaining pastry over filling; press down firmly.

Left to right: Cottage-Cheese Konafa, Cheese & Eggplant Flan

Mediterranean Cheese Roll

1/4 cup butter or margarine
1/2 cup finely chopped onion
2 tablespoons toasted bread crumbs
1/4 cup chopped fresh coriander
2 tablespoons grated lemon peel
1 egg
1 (8-oz.) pkg. cream cheese or Neufchâtel cheese, room temperature
8 oz. filo dough (10 sheets), thawed if frozen
1/2 cup butter or margarine, melted

1. Preheat oven to 400F (205C). Grease a large baking sheet. Melt butter or margarine in a small saucepan. Add onion; sauté until transparent, stirring occasionally.
2. Stir in bread crumbs, coriander and lemon peel; sauté 1 to 2 minutes; set aside.

3. In a medium bowl, beat egg and cheese until light and fluffy. Stir in onion-and-crumb mixture.
4. Unfold filo sheets; cover with a slightly damp towel. Place a dry towel on a flat surface. Lay 1 filo sheet on towel; brush with melted butter or margarine. Place another filo sheet next to first sheet, overlapping edges by 2-1/2 inches. Brush second sheet with melted butter or margarine. Top with remaining 8 filo sheets, arranging in same way. Brush each 1 with melted butter or margarine.
5. Spread filling over filo to within 1 inch of edges. Fold edges of filo over filling. Using towel and starting from 1 short end, carefully roll up filled pastry.
6. Use towel to place filled roll, seam-side down, on greased baking sheet. Brush with melted butter or margarine.
7. Bake in preheated oven 40 minutes or until puffed and golden brown. Serve hot. Makes 4 to 6 servings.

Mushroom & Cheese Pizza

1-1/2 cups shredded Cheddar cheese (6 oz.)
1 tablespoon all-purpose flour
Pinch of salt
1 teaspoon freshly ground pepper
2 eggs
1 tablespoon kirsch
1 tablespoon butter or margarine
1/3 cup chopped onion
1 (8-oz.) can tomatoes, drained, chopped
2 cups sliced fresh mushrooms
1 cup chopped cooked ham
1-1/2 tablespoons chopped fresh parsley or coriander
1 recipe Biscuit Pizza Dough, opposite

1. Preheat oven to 400F (205C). Grease 2 baking sheets. In a medium bowl, combine cheese, flour, salt and pepper. Beat in eggs, 1 at a time, beating well after each addition. Beat in kirsch; let stand 10 minutes.
2. Melt butter or margarine in a small pan over low heat. Add onion; sauté 5 minutes to soften, stirring occasionally. Stir sautéed onion, tomatoes, mushrooms, ham and parsley or coriander into cheese mixture until combined.
3. Make and roll out dough into circles as directed opposite. Spread each circle with 1/4 of filling.
4. Bake in preheated oven 20 to 25 minutes or until crust is crisp and filling is bubbly. Serve hot. Makes 4 servings.

Variation
Italian-Style Pizza: Substitute mozzarella cheese for Cheddar cheese, 6 chopped anchovy fillets for ham and 2 teaspoons oregano for parsley or coriander. Complete as above, omitting salt.

Mushroom & Cheese Pizzas

Biscuit Pizza Dough

1-2/3 cups self-rising flour
1 teaspoon baking powder
1/2 cup shredded Cheddar cheese or mozzarella cheese (2 oz.)
2 tablespoons butter or margarine
2/3 cup milk

1. Grease a large baking sheet.
2. In a medium bowl, combine flour, baking powder and cheese. With a pastry blender or 2 knives, cut in butter or margarine until mixture resembles coarse crumbs.
3. Stir in milk to make a soft dough. Knead dough on a lightly floured surface until smooth.
4. Divide dough in fourths. On a lightly floured surface, roll or pat out each piece to a 6-inch circle. Place on greased baking sheet. Use for Mushroom & Cheese Pizza, opposite, or use favorite topping. Bake as directed in recipe for Mushroom & Cheese Pizza. Makes 4 (6-inch) pizzas.

Three-Cheese Spinach Tart

1/2 (10-oz.) pkg. frozen chopped spinach, thawed, drained
1 cup cottage cheese, drained
1 cup shredded Monterey Jack cheese (4 oz.)
1/3 cup grated Parmesan cheese (1 oz.)
1 egg, beaten
Freshly ground nutmeg
Freshly ground pepper
1 (9-inch) unbaked pastry shell, page 8

1. Preheat oven to 375F (190C).
2. In a medium bowl, combine spinach, cottage cheese, 3/4 cup Monterey Jack cheese, Parmesan cheese and egg. Season with nutmeg and pepper.
3. Spoon spinach mixture into pastry shell. Smooth top; sprinkle with remaining 1/4 cup Monterey Jack cheese.
4. Bake in preheated oven about 45 minutes or until crust is brown and filling bubbles. Cool in pan on a wire rack 5 minutes. Cut into wedges to serve. Makes 6 servings.

Mozzarella & Tomato Tart

1/2 (17-1/2-oz.) pkg. frozen puff pastry (1 sheet), thawed
2 large tomatoes, cut into 1/2-inch slices, seeded
2-1/2 tablespoons olive oil
1/2 teaspoon salt
1/2 teaspoon freshly ground pepper
1 tablespoon Dijon-style mustard
8 oz. mozzarella cheese, cut into 1/4-inch slices
2 tablespoons chopped fresh coriander or 1 tablespoon dried leaf coriander

To garnish:
Fresh coriander leaves

Olive oil, tomatoes and fresh coriander give this recipe a marked flavor of Provence. Serve tart as a delicious summer supper dish.

1. Preheat oven to 375F (190C). Grease an 8-inch springform pan.
2. Unfold pastry. On a lightly floured surface, roll out pastry into a 12-inch square. Cut out a 12-inch circle. Use pastry to line bottom and side of greased pan. Prick all over with a fork. Chill.
3. Meanwhile place tomato slices on a large plate; brush slices with olive oil. Sprinkle with salt and pepper; let stand 15 minutes, turning occasionally.
4. Spread mustard over chilled pastry bottom. Arrange mozzarella cheese over bottom; sprinkle with 1/2 of coriander. Arrange seasoned tomato slices over cheese; pour any tomato juices over tomatoes. Sprinkle with remaining coriander.
5. Bake in preheated oven 40 to 50 minutes or until pastry is golden brown. Cool in pan on a wire rack 15 minutes.
6. Carefully remove side of pan; place on a serving plate. Garnish with coriander leaves. Serve lukewarm. Makes 4 servings.

Index